Mostly Rapscallions

Salient Sillies about the Rich and the Infamous in History

P. J. Sullivan

Revised and Updated
Unauthorized Uncut Uncensored Uncouth

Copyright © 2010 by P. J. Sullivan

ISBN 978-0-7414-6167-4

Printed in the United States of America

Published June 2013

INFINITY PUBLISHING
1094 New DeHaven Street, Suite 100
West Conshohocken, PA 19428-2713
Toll-free (877) BUY BOOK
Local Phone (610) 941-9999
Fax (610) 941-9959
Info@buybooksontheweb.com
www.buybooksontheweb.com

Those in power must spend a lot of their time laughing at us.

—ALICE WALKER

No matter how cynical you get, it's almost impossible to keep up.

—LILY TOMLIN

If you don't know history, it is as if you were born yesterday.

—HOWARD ZINN

Contents

Acknowledgments i

Introduction iii

Part I: Religious Wackos.................................... 1

   * THE BORGIAS 3

   * THE SPANISH INQUISITION........................ 14

   * OLIVER CROMWELL 23

   * ANTHONY COMSTOCK 31

Part II: Damyanks...39

   * ANDREW JACKSON 41

   * U. S. GRANT....................................50

   * WOODROW WILSON.................................59

   * WILLIAM RANDOLPH HEARST 67

Part III: Bloodsuckers................................. 75

   * IVAN THE TERRIBLE 77

   * PIRATES.......................................86

   * BOSS TWEED....................................95

   * JOHN D. ROCKEFELLER........................... 103

Part IV: Jacks and Queens 111

   * SIR WALTER RALEGH...........................113

   * MARIE ANTOINETTE 122

   * BISMARCK....................................131

   * QUEEN VICTORIA.............................. 139

Part V: Imperialist Warmongers 147

    * HERNAN CORTES 149

    * ROBERT CLIVE 157

    * NAPOLEON BONAPARTE 165

    * CECIL RHODES 173

Part VI: Popular Hate Figures 181

    * KAISER WILHELM II 183

    * BENITO MUSSOLINI 191

    * ADOLF HITLER 199

    * FRANCISCO FRANCO 208

Part VII: Weirdos and Worse 217

    * GILLES DE RAIS 219

    * CASANOVA 227

    * HETTY GREEN 236

    * RASPUTIN 244

About Sources 253

Picture Sources 255

About the Author 259

Acknowledgments

This book was distilled from library resources at Humboldt State University, Arcata, California, and the Humboldt County, California, library system. Thanks also to local bookstores, such as the Tin Can Mailman, and to Amazon.com for hard-to-find books not available locally. Thanks to Nancy Burns, Casey Meaden, and Bob Oswell for computer advice and support. Thanks to Aaron Shepard for his excellent manual on book layout. Thanks to Marian Claassen for lending me a book by Kaiser Wilhelm's dentist, to Richard Sahn for his mordant observations on human society, and to Monica Sahn for suggesting that I include a chapter about Hernan Cortes. Thanks to Dr. Stephen Bantz for feedback, to the late Peter Lumsden for showing me England, and to Joan Ryan for her hospitality in Spain. Thanks to Mirrorpix for permission to use the image of Mussolini. And thanks to the inimitable Will Cuppy (1884-1949) for proving beyond reasonable doubt that learning history can be fun.

Introduction

Why this book? Why not? What better way to learn history than from the scoundrels who made it? Of course, not all movers and shakers have been scoundrels, but if you study the scoundrels you won't miss much. History was a bloody business. Benito Mussolini said, "It is only blood that makes the wheels of history turn." He should have known; he turned a few. "All kings is mostly rapscallions," said the great American philosopher Huckleberry Finn.

"Laughter is the enemy of tyranny," said Howard Zinn. What better way to deal with tyrants and bullies than by laughing them out of town? From a safe distance, of course. So I have carefully hidden one laugh in each chapter of this book. At least a chuckle. Trust me, it is there. You might have to read the footnotes, but it should not be necessary to read between the lines. If you still can't find it, then remember the immortal words of Edgar Johnson, "Satire need not be funny."

"So long as men worship the Caesars and Napoleons," said Aldous Huxley, "Caesars and Napoleons will duly arise and make them miserable." Yes, but if you laugh at them, the Caesars and Napoleons will duly slink into the woodwork, where they belong. Tyrants cannot take a joke. They can dish it out, but not take it. Mussolini flipped his lid at the merest hint of ridicule. Napoleon truly feared only one man, the cartoonist James Gillray. "*Figaro* destroyed the aristocracy," said Beaumarchais.

I would like to apologize to Asia, Africa, Australia, and South America for not including their rapscallions in this book. I did not mean to imply that their most despicable were not good enough—or bad enough—to be included. Mostly they were just not in the right place at the right time. Or was it the wrong place at the wrong time? Anyway, no slight was intended. I'm sure their worst could compete with ours in a fair contest of depravity. Feel free to laugh at them on your own time, but my time and space are limited. I did mention one Chinese pirate, after all.

Some have asked, why not include up-to-date scoundrels from the twenty-first century? Don't we have some whoppers today? Indeed we do, but I will leave them to future historians. Let them ferment a bit with time. Remember what I said about a safe distance. Sir Walter Ralegh said, "Whosoever in writing a modern history shall follow the truth too near its heels, it may haply strike out his teeth." As Sir Walter found out the hard way, getting saucy with the powerful can be hazardous to one's health and longevity unless they, and their in-laws, are a few generations removed.

And if my rants should cause offense to your favorite minority group, please understand that I have made every effort to distribute offenses equitably. If I have gored your favorite ox, it was not the only one, so don't take it personally. Satire is a kind of licensed bad form, said Edgar Johnson. Nothing wrong with a little bad form in a good cause, especially when you've got the goods on someone. If Pollyanna and Dr. Pangloss are your heroes, you might want to reconsider whether you really need to read this book.

So many scoundrels, so little time. It is the aim of this book to demote these few a little closer to their rightful places in history. But enough of this! Let's get on with the story and the search for laughs. Happy hunting!

P. J. Sullivan

I

Religious Wackos

The Borgias

The Spanish Inquisition

Oliver Cromwell

Anthony Comstock

Pope Alexander VI

The Borgias

The trouble began in 1455, when Alfonso de Borja became Pope Calixtus III. His Borja relatives came swarming in from Spain like a plague of locusts, seeking papal plums, honors, power, pleasure—mainly a good time. Pope Calixtus opened the door and let the Borjas in.[1]

He took care of his *nepoti,* especially his favorite nephew Rodrigo, a bright youth who loved pleasure. Rodrigo was a ladies' man. His behavior with them was said to be "excessive." Always smiling as if up to something, he usually was. He was built like a battering ram, but had a honeyed tongue. Although not the stuff of

---

[1] Spaniards like the Borjas were cordially detested in Italy so they Italianized their names to Borgia. It didn't fool anybody.

which clerics are made, he took a vow of celibacy and became Cardinal Borgia. But alas, the vow did not take, and soon "natural" children were showing up out of nowhere. They all looked like Borgias. In fact, they all looked like Rodrigo Borgia. He looked after them, in his fashion, from a safe distance.

At age fifty-eight, Cardinal Borgia became hopelessly besotted with fifteen-year-old Giulia Farnese, an acclaimed cutie. It was not mutual. In fact, he had to threaten her with excommunication and eternal damnation to keep her away from "that monkey, that stallion," her lawful husband. Historians will never agree about the paternity of little Laura, who was born to Giulia about 1492. She looked a lot like Rodrigo, but so did lots of other kids. You can't make a case out of her Borgia nose because Giulia's lawful husband, Orso Orsini, also had a Borgia nose. So only the recording angel knows for sure. By 1500 Giulia was free, as she was over the hill at age twenty-six. Rodrigo was sixty-nine, going on twenty.

Cardinal Borgia saved up his ducats and bought the papacy in 1492, calling himself Pope Alexander VI. As pope he wanted to be "father to all men," but for the ladies he had other plans. Although the purchase price is unknown, rumor had it that he bought the papacy at the price of his soul, plus change. Sorry, I don't know how much his soul was worth. Pope Alexander's aims were: always to be on the side of the strong, and to enrich his bastards—those he could keep track of. And of course, to have a good time.

There were many ways popes could get money in those days and he tried them all: taxing Jews, selling indulgences, pocketing crusade funds, selling red hats and papal bulls, mining alum. A royal divorce could be worth twenty-five thousand ducats. He found that by selling heavenly bliss at competitive prices he could balance the church budget, with plenty left over for parties and good times. Alex tried to reform the church, but his reforms never got very far. People wondered why he didn't just settle for reforming himself.

A dinner invitation from Pope Alex was a dubious matter. Not only was the food frugal, but there was the Borgia reputation to be considered, as they were rumored to be competent poisoners.[2] If you got him into the right mood, His Holiness might let you kiss the pontifical feet, in lieu of dessert. If you were a cardinal, you could even kiss him on the lips and call it dessert.

King Charles VIII of France[3] decided to reform the church by removing its head. In 1494 he invaded Rome and put a stop to the fun for a while. Pope Alex hated him so much that he refused to let him kiss his feet! In time he repulsed the French by displaying the heads of Saints Peter and Paul, which had seen better days. The French also failed to reform the church. Meanwhile, Martin Luther was in town for the jubilee in 1500 and didn't miss a thing.

In 1503 Pope Alex died and seven devils came to claim his soul. They had first dibs on it. A deal was a deal, after all. His funeral was interrupted by a donnybrook and followed by widespread looting. He left many legacies, including uncounted bastards, the stink of abomination, and the Protestant Reformation. He also introduced bullfighting to Rome.[4] He was the origin of the age-old question: "Is the pope a Catholic?" Alex should be judged in context. Today we would find it unseemly for a pope to throw sweets into the low-cut bodices of ladies' gowns, but remember that His Holiness was a man of the Renaissance. In those days a pope was allowed a little fun. Alex had a fool named Gabrieletto, a Catalan. Personally, I have never felt the need for a fool.

Cesare Borgia was probably one of Pope Alexander's bastards, but he liked to think of himself as destiny's

---

[2] Baron Corvo says Pope Alexander's murders "fail of proof." He wonders where he would have found the time.

[3] The one with twelve toes and the enormous beak nose.

[4] The bull killed two people, but the Romans loved it.

child. He made everybody nervous, including his father. You wouldn't want to have him over for dinner. Cesare was hungry for power, not just for a good time. He was all business.[5] Cesare was a bastard until 1480, when a papal bull declared that he was not. Later he became a bastard again to escape religious vows. Eventually he became an insufferable bastard, end of discussion. The pope had power to legitimize bastards, change people's parentage, and even create virgins out of ladies of the night. His papal bulls were infallibly true, even when they were not. But he could not cure Cesare's pox—the French disease, you know.

And speaking of the French, Cesare decided to subdue them by marrying into them. His marriage to Charlotte d'Albret, sister of the king of Navarre, was a love match, as they both loved money and power. Cesare claimed he made "eight trips" on their wedding night, but did not say where he went. We will probably never know for sure. They had a homely but somewhat legitimate child, Luisa. The rest of his children were more "natural" than most. Cesare was not a family man; he had a career to attend to, so he left before Luisa was born, never to return. He did not forget her, however, as he married her off at age three. Luisa turned out to be pious and gentle. She must have been a mutation.

Although a cardinal from an early age and a cardinal sinner from even earlier, Cesare never had any desire to be a priest, so he renounced his red hat and was secularized in 1498. Not interested in crusading against infidel Turks, he preferred to slaughter Christians closer to home. He had grandiose plans for a Borgian kingdom all his own, his very own extortion racket, paying tribute to him, not to Rome. But in the meantime, he needed the safety of his father's skirts.

---

[5] Except for one hobby: debauchery.

Cesare gave his marching orders when his astrologers told him the time was right.[6] He came to be known as "the Scourge of Italy," and why not? It suited him. A ruthless despot, he believed in swift justice or, if necessary, swift injustice. He was like an American, always talking of peace and preparing for war.

Although piety was at low ebb when he was born, Cesare has been criticized for murdering so many people. A few should have been sufficient, but he had a professional executioner and a chemist on his payroll, and they both needed to keep in practice. The former, Michelotto, specialized in strangling; the latter, Sebastian, in poisoning. Either way, they got the job done. The Borgia reputation for poisoning is overrated, however. If they were such competent poisoners, why did he need a strangler on his payroll? Sometimes they even had to resort to daggers. Pietro Torrigiani joined Cesare's court for a while, a sculptor whose résumé included breaking Michelangelo's nose.

The air in Rome was said to be "insalubrious," but it was not the air. It was Cesare. You could always tell when he was in town, by the corpses floating in the Tiber. There was talk. In a fit of temper, Pope Alexander once called Cesare a "son of a bitch," but he didn't really mean it and never said it again. Besides, it probably sounded better in Spanish.[7] Cesare's mother was probably Vannozza Cattanei, or Big Jenny, a Roman woman who was respectably married at the time, though not to Cesare's father. Pope Alex once had someone hanged for calling his "natural" son Juan "a priest's bastard," which doesn't seem quite fair.

According to Niccolo Machiavelli, a Florentine spy, Cesare always had good reasons for his crimes. "The duke was only carrying out the law," said Baron Corvo. If

_____

[6] The time was right when his bankers told his astrologers there was enough money available.
[7] When upset, he would lapse into Spanish.

people did not want their tongues or hands cut off, why did they write epigrams about Cesare? But attempts at rehabilitating Cesare's memory are pointless. He was Machiavellian. In fact, he was the model for *The Prince*, Machiavelli's how-to book on the art of killing and exploiting people for their own good. Cesare was cruel, but it was OK, said Machiavelli, because being nice did not work on Italians, or on the French either. Besides, there was no nice way to cut throats. There still isn't, to this day. Cesare would exterminate those who opposed him and things would be quiet for a while. After wiping up the blood, his subjects could get back to pursuing the Italian dream, even to living happily ever after, until the next bloodbath. Wouldn't you settle for that? Cesare imposed what was then believed to be law and order.

When his daddy died in 1503, Cesare's peaceable kingdom erupted in rebellion and the new pope arrested him. So much for his dreams of glory and payoffs! "His sins have found him out," said Machiavelli, who had once admired those sins.[8] Cesare died in exile, in Spain, before the Inquisition could catch up with him. Now boiling in the seventh circle of the inferno, he has become an object of abuse to history. Let that be a lesson to you the next time you are inclined to try Machiavelli's program.

Lucretia Borgia, another of Pope Alexander's bastards, was not as bad as you think. She was not even especially depraved, for a Borgia, despite her reputation for lewdness and associating with disreputable people like the pope. She might not even have poisoned anybody! She didn't even want to meddle in politics. Mainly she just wanted to have a good time. Is that so bad? It wasn't her fault when her husbands slipped away on fast horses, in fear for their lives. But she did support her murderous brother more than was strictly necessary, as if she actually wanted to. She even danced with him, and didn't

---

[8] Machiavelli said it is safer to be feared than loved. Especially if you happen to be unlovable, as he was.

seem to mind that he had murdered her husband and possibly her brother. She "may not have had a very clearly defined opinion of her brother," said Gregorovius. Bellonci says Lucretia had a "heavily charged past" already at age nineteen but no problem, her father could make her a virgin with the stroke of a pen. This was one of the perks that came with being the daughter of a pope. Lucretia may have been the first female pope. When her father was away on business, or more likely on pleasure, she got to play at being in charge of the Vatican. But she was not infallible.

Lucretia Borgia

She was much criticized for taking a daily bath. It was considered immoral to take baths, as the heathen Moors did. There must be Moorish blood in her, complained the locals, but I am inclined to forgive her for the baths, as she probably meant no harm by them.

Her marriages were arranged by her father and her brother for "practical considerations." When her first marriage became impractical, Lucretia was declared a virgin in order to annul it. Naturally, this set all Italy to laughing.[9] Meanwhile her husband, who couldn't see the humor in it, beat the odds and escaped with his life. He was no bargain anyway.

Hubby was long gone when a mysterious baby occurred in Lucretia's bedroom. To this day, nobody knows where it came from. It may have been Lucretia's "natural" child by a lackey who was found floating in the Tiber about that time, or it might have been the pope's child or Cesare's. Or was it brought by a stork? The public didn't know whether Lucretia was the pope's daughter or wife or niece or daughter-in-law or sugar baby or all of the above. It was a mess, so in 1501 the pope decided to clear up the confusion with two papal bulls. The first declared the child was Cesare's by an unnamed Roman woman.[10] The second declared the child was the pope's own offspring. Strange to say, these two bulls failed to settle the matter. Perhaps the pope did not know himself who was the baby's father. But the little one had a Borgia nose and inherited lots of goodies. It later became the Duke of Nepi and passed as Lucretia's brother.

Lucretia's second husband, Alfonso of Aragon, was young and cute but soon dead, probably by the strangler on Cesare's payroll, who said the pope was behind it. The crimes of father and son were always getting confused; I've given up trying to sort them out. Her second marriage had gotten off to a bad start anyway, as two

---

[9] She was six months pregnant at the time.
[10] Lucretia was a Roman woman, but she had a name.

bishops were beaten up during the wedding festivities. Even in those days, this sort of thing was considered bad form.

As her first two husbands had been so "unlucky," Lucretia was reluctant to marry again, but her third husband had a quality that she found irresistible: he lived a long way from Rome, in Ferrara. Alfonso d'Este was reluctant, uncouth, palsied, dour, mostly absent, and eccentric to the point of lunacy. He had squalid habits. The word *squalid* was invented for the likes of him. All he cared about were whores and cannons. Although her marriage had been bought and paid for, Lucretia felt unwanted in Ferrara. Her stingy new father-in-law expected her to live on a measly ten thousand ducats a year. Her new sister-in-law Isabella was too wonderful for words, and didn't she know it! No wonder Isabella's husband flirted with Lucretia. Prima donna to the world, Isabella wanted no competition from a mere pope's bastard. Isabella "was so legitimate that it hurt," said Will Cuppy. Lucretia should have been welcome in Ferrara as insurance against her monstrous brother, but he visited her, which freaked everybody out.

So, love-starved on the malarial plains of Ferrara, Lucretia turned to poetry or, more precisely, to poets. They had such lovely ways of courting her. Could she help it that her favorite poems were about her? You'll have to decide for yourself whether Lucretia and Pietro Bembo became lovers, as I was not there to take notes. No doubt he was an ardent swain who could flatter her in Greek and Latin meter. His letters were mushy, even for love letters, but Her Ladyship did not seem to mind. We don't know how far they went. Marital infidelity was punishable by beheading, according to a quaint custom in the family, and they both kept their heads. He did deem it advisable, however, to skip town when Alfonso became jealous. Smart move! No doubt Bembo was smitten, but with ambition, not with her. His poems were dedicated to her, but secretly inspired by other women. Will Cuppy notes that Lucretia's poet friends tended to show up at mealtimes.

When her other poet friend, Ercole Strozzi, was found suspiciously dead one morning it must have seemed like old times to Lucretia, but this time it was not Cesare who did it. He had a good alibi—he was sizzling in hell at the time. Some suspect Alfonso, but who knows? It is hard to know who did it because the murder suited so many people. Ariosto was another poet who flattered Lucretia beyond the call of duty. When Isabella's husband, Francesco Gonzaga,[11] flirted with Lucretia, it was mutual. Whether they ever transgressed the bounds of propriety is anyone's guess, but Ercole Strozzi told Francesco that if he went to her he would "achieve what he desired," love's final aim.[12] So did he go to her? I'll leave that one to your imaginations, and to the doctoral theses. In 1508 Lucretia produced a male heir and it must have looked more like Alfonso than Francesco because the Estes finally decided she was like family—an Este for keeps!

As I said, infidelity was punishable by beheading in the Este family. Why then did Lucretia's marriage contract say that she would have to give back her jewels if she cheated on Alfonso? Wasn't that a bit redundant? What good is a necklace to someone who has no neck?

Lucretia turned to religion, often disappearing into convents to do retreats or have babies. She loved solitude, and no wonder! It was said that she wore hair shirts beneath her court dresses, but I don't know why she would think that necessary. Being married to Alfonso was penance enough to cover anybody's sins.

She did not have a hard schedule. Winter was the festive season and spring to autumn was vacation time. I could handle that myself!

---

[11] He had the pox, you know.
[12] And she would achieve his pox.

She has been criticized for being so submissive to her father and her brother, but could you have done any better? At least she survived to the ripe old age of thirty-nine. By the way, she wrote her name Lucretia, not Lucrezia. Of course, she might have been mistaken.

There were lots of other Borgias, but you needn't keep track of them. Reliable information about Borgias is hard to come by and, as Pope Pius II said, "Shame forbids mention of all that took place." Much that we know about the Borgias comes from Burchard's sacristan's book, which had to be written with great discretion, as it was accessible to the Borgias. So we are getting the censored version!

Borgias are popular with people who like whodunnits, moot points, and heated arguments because no one will ever know for sure who their fathers were or who did what to whom. Despite the enduring popularity of the family sins, one Borgia tried so hard to atone for them that he became a saint. Saint Francis Borgia died trying in 1572.

If you should ever find yourself at table with a Borgia, ask for a doggie bag, but be discreet about it.

The Spanish Inquisition

The Spanish Inquisition was known as "the Holy Office" because it was holier than thou. It tried to exterminate heresy by exterminating heretics, especially pushy heretics with attitude problems. It was the duty of Christians to kill heretics, especially Jews, before they infected others.[13] Nevermind that Jesus was a Jew. Why bring that up?

Heretics were like weeds in your garden, and the Holy Office was a kind of spiritual Roundup. What would *you* do with them? You could banish them, but to where? Most places already had enough heretics and didn't need any more.

Heretics were people who disagreed with the Holy Office. They were all over Spain, spreading like colds in a

---

[13] Killing heretics could get you a plenary indulgence.

kindergarten. Babies sucked in heresy with their mothers' milk. Even some of the popes were heretics. It could happen to anybody.[14]

Jews in Spain were believed to be Judaizing. That is what Jews did, and still do, whether you like it or not. Especially Jews who had been forced into the bosom of the church at the point of a sword. Jews clashed with the Christian motif of Spain, so they were expelled, minus their money and property, and became wandering Jews. If they agreed to convert and blend in with the decor, they could stay. Well, maybe.

But even when they converted, how could you be sure that Jews were not still Judaizing when nobody was watching? Backsliding, circumcising themselves in private, eating meat during Lent, or changing their clothes on Saturdays? Could you trust people with names like Moshe, Mordechai, Levi, Hanna, or Zipora to be good Catholics? Conversion of Jews was never final; it had to be constantly enforced. So the Inquisition established tribunals all over Spain to keep a watchful eye on the Jews, especially Jews who had money or property that could be put to better use.

"Converted" Jews were known as *Conversos,* new Christians, crypto-Judaizers, phonies, or closet heretics. Real Christians were called old Christians, good guys, or *Limpios,* the Clean Ones, although they hardly ever bathed. The Spanish Inquisition concerned itself mainly with uppity *Conversos* who thought they were as good as real Spaniards, just because they had been baptized. Canon law recognized their baptisms, but no one else did. Baptism of Jews was only skin deep, if it took at all. Even a sacrament had to have something to work with! Peter the Venerable argued that Jews should be afflicted with fearful torments until they had given up their bad habits

---

[14] Most people went to hell in those days. You needed contacts to get into the other place.

15

forever. I mean really, for keeps! Friendly persuasion did not work on Jews.

Occasionally innocent people were mistakenly killed by the secular arm of the Inquisition, but this was not a problem because, as Christian martyrs, they would proceed directly to paradise without passing GO. Not a bad deal, actually. Paradise is a nice place, I hear tell. Nice beaches, virgins everywhere, rent control, no death or taxes. Wouldn't you settle for that? But I digress. The Inquisition tried to be fair. Pregnant women were spared, for example, until they had given birth.[15]

Heresy, in those days, took many forms:
* refusing to eat pork,
* refusing to serve customers on Saturdays,
* believing that the sun was the center of the solar system,
* peeing against the walls of a church,
* reading heathen authors, such as Voltaire,
* having scars where the tail was removed,
* denying that the Messiah had come,
* knowing the Old Testament too well,
* smiling at mention of the Virgin Mary,
* telling Jesus jokes,
* eating with Jews,
* eating bread without the yeast,
* grieving over the death of a Jew,
* thinking bad thoughts,
* comparing Inquisitors unfavorably with the devil.

Be honest now, how many of these have you been guilty of? Fornication and adultery were gray areas, usually not considered heretical unless you believed in them. Besides, some of the Inquisitors and popes were fond of them. Bigamy was another gray area. Depravity was OK, but not heretical depravity.

---

[15] Their babies were given to real Christians, who could watch them for signs of Judaizing.

A woman was burned at the stake for saying that the Holy Office was more interested in confiscating property than in saving souls, which doesn't seem quite fair because in 1483 the pope said the same thing and got away with it. But Inquisitors did try to keep a proper love/hate balance. They did try to hate Jews more than they loved their possessions.

You might have heard that the Inquisition burned people. Well, it is not true; it only "relaxed" them to the secular arm. Did it know what the secular arm would do with them? Could it read minds? Of course, some heretics got so "relaxed" that they never moved again, but the Holy Office abhorred bloodshed. There were strict rules of procedure. Repeating tortures, for example, was forbidden. However, there was nothing wrong with resuming them. No pain, no gain was the policy.

Some argue that we should not judge the Inquisition by modern standards of morality. Sure, we know now that torturing and relaxing people are not nice things to do, but how were Inquisitors to know that in those dark days? Did they have Dr. Laura to give them moral advice? Or Dr. Phil? Could they write to Ann Landers? Why did God make hell if burning people was a no-no? Only one heretic in fifty was burned by the secular arm, said Coultman. That's not a bad average—if you were among the forty-nine. Burning heretics was not always necessary; cutting out their tongues would sometimes suffice. Inquisitors were God-fearing men. That was the problem. They were afraid that heretics would bring down the wrath of God upon them all.

About 1474, printing presses began appearing in Spain, followed by a spate of heretical catechisms, vulgar bibles, Talmuds, and God knows what else! The bonfires of the Holy Office rose to the challenge.

The most notable inquisitor was Tomás de Torquemada, also known as "the Saintly One" or "the Lord's Jew Roaster." Some say that his grandfather was a Jew, but offending ancestors could be expunged, for a fee.[16] Torquemada liked to burn books as well as Jews. His other hobby was wearing the latest in hair shirts. It was Torquemada who organized the Holy Office into a lean, mean, cleansing machine.

Torquemada

Cardinal Ximenes was much like Torquemada. A pious man, he was especially proud of his humility. Having subdued his own flesh, he set out to subdue the flesh of others, believing that penance was more effectual when it selflessly reached out to include others. Ximenes would have enjoyed being pallid and wasted if he had been capable of enjoyment at all. All he wanted from life was a simple hermitage, a supply of hair shirts, and a

---

[16] You were nobody in those days unless you had your own genealogist.

floor to sleep on. Instead he was made an archbishop, and then the governing of Spain descended upon him. He accepted these irksome duties because he believed that happiness was a sin; that's all you need to know about him. Admonished by the pope to dress like a proper bishop, he wore hair shirts under his episcopal robes and slept on the floor, next to his magnificent episcopal bed. He believed that bigotry was a virtue because his god was a bigot. Ximenes decided to do to the heathen Moors what Torquemada had done to the Jews. Baptism or exile was his program.

Luteranismo began seeping into Spain from up north. Lutherans did not Judaize, but were heretics just the same. So were Jansenists, humanists, the Portuguese, and just about anybody else who was not especially nice. The Duke of Alva, a military agent of the Holy Office in Flanders, wanted to exterminate the entire Dutch nation because it was Protestant. He killed eighteen thousand Dutch heathens, but it was a big job. He was recalled to Spain because it was costing too much money. The duke outdid Torquemada and Ximenes in killing, but never caught on in the history books as they did. I guess he lacked their charisma.

But Jews were the main problem. They were known to crucify redeemers,[17] cause plagues, eat garlic, ravish nuns. They threw Christians down wells, collected taxes for the king, changed their underwear on Fridays, threw stones at crosses on Good Friday. They were in league with the Sultan of Turkey. They turned Christians into mad dogs, hexed Christian churches, stabbed Communion wafers until they spurted blood. They multiplied themselves. Worst of all, they prospered. Now do you agree that something had to be done about the Jews?

The Moors and *Moriscos* (converted Moors) were not much better. They prayed with their faces facing east,

---

[17] To be fair, I have never actually seen a Jew crucify a redeemer. They don't do it often.

took baths public and private, stained their nails with henna, spoke Arabic, plotted with Turks, and undercut the wages of Spanish workers.[18] They preferred Mahomet to Jesus. And the bribes they offered were woefully inadequate.

By 1550 there were only two kinds of people in Spain: Catholics and liars, but their fortunes declined without the Moors, who had done most of the work, and the Jews, who had paid most of the taxes. People began to wonder whether the Holy Office was such a good idea after all. But they didn't wonder out loud!

Mystics, lunatics, and holy fools were usually tolerated, just in case they might turn out to be saints, unless of course they dabbled in politics or insisted on defending their ridiculous views. People who defended their views were considered unrepentent.

Witches were poor, so there was little financial incentive to bother them. They messed with the weather, which upset farmers, and sucked blood out of children, which was generally frowned upon, but witchcraft was often considered a secular matter, outside the jurisdiction of the Inquisition. Sure, it was annoying to see witches flying through the air, but was it heretical? They had disgusting habits, such as digging up corpses and eating them, but was it heretical?

Dead people were not safe from the Inquisition either. Sometimes heretical corpses were disinterred, processed, and punished. There was no need to "relax" them, however. Corpses without property were left to rest in peace. What would be the point? Children were not safe either, especially precocious children who could Judaize beyond their years.

After being tried, if you can call it that, the condemned were publicly displayed at autos-de-fe, so the

---

[18] In one parish, Moriscos asked for the priest to be removed because all their children were being born with blue eyes like his.

righteous could be suitably edified by their distress. Autos were good shows, if your mind twisted that way, with lots of ritual, pageantry, lamentations, high drama, low drama, overacting, etc. Something for every taste. There wasn't much else to do in those days. Autos lasted all day—bring a picnic lunch. Afterwards, the secular arm did its thing. Toasting heretics was not unlike toasting marshmallows, only more so.

By about 1750, the Inquisition had run out of human fuel, but there were books to be burned. Censorship became its focus. In time, Napoleon and his brother Joseph looted it dry. The French relegated the Holy Office to the dustbin of history—for a while—but it still pops up now and again in different guises. Don't count it out. So-called Christians still kill more people than the Romans did. What was Generalisimo Franco but a born-again Inquisitor? And Mr. Hitler had rather strong opinions about Jews. My own neighbors are too inquisitive.

If a tribunal should set up in your neighborhood, consider renaming your dog Ximenes, but otherwise don't drop names. Claiming to be sixth cousin, twice removed, to the Holy Spirit will get you nowhere. I wouldn't worry too much about it. These days you are more likely to be run over by a bus. In those days, there were no busses. If heretics get to be a problem in your neighborhood, there are African tribal masks designed to keep evil spirits away. Just put one on your front door, underneath your NRA[19] sticker. But remember, most heretics are just folks, once you get to know them.

Despite the wealth it sucked out of Jews, the Inquisition barely broke even. It had expenses. Executioners didn't come cheap. Carpenters, firewood, stakes, refreshments, publicity, porta potties, racks, whips, iron virgins, all had to be paid for. It got no grants from the Ford Foundation, no spin-offs. It couldn't even sell T-shirts. So if you are thinking of starting a tribunal in your neighborhood, consider the economics, if nothing else.[20] It is not the way to get ahead. Run like a franchise, the Inquisition closed branch tribunals and moved on, like an ideological vacuum cleaner, when districts had been suitably cleansed. Are there enough undesirables in your neighborhood to justify a tribunal? Do they have any money? If not, are you willing to relocate? Hey, it isn't easy! Why not just sell vacuum cleaners? Times have changed. Relaxing Protestants is no longer socially acceptable. These days it won't even get you a plenary indulgence.

The Inquisition failed to abolish heresy. To this day there are people who believe that the sun is the center of our solar system.

---

19 National Rifle Association
20 Most instruction manuals for Inquisitors are now out-of-date. Hair shirts are hard to find on eBay.

Oliver Cromwell

Oliver Cromwell lived in the seventeenth century, if you can call it living. Known as "the Old Killjoy," he believed it was sinful to have fun, especially on the Sabbath. It was sinful to dance, leap about, slide on ice, paint faces, play cards, roll dice—everything that made life worth living in those days. Royalists claimed that he had his fill of fun in his youth, gaming, tippling, and wenching, but that was before he became a born-again killjoy. Although a Puritan, Oliver was never a bluenose, as he had a prominent red nose. "The glow worm glistened in his beak."

Little is known about his private life, and that might be a good thing. He had a large family. There was some disagreement about his wife. She was frugal, said those partial to parliamentary government; she was stingy, said royalists. You decide, but be advised: never dine with a

Cromwell on an empty stomach. Oliver was almost a gentleman, although he occasionally did an honest day's work. He was keenly aware that his family fortune had been stolen from Papists during the reign of Henry VIII. He did not want to give it back so naturally he distrusted uppity Papists and monarchs who were soft on popery.[21]

Oliver was forever fretting about his soul, fearing that there was a space reserved for it in the infernal regions. So, with the money he saved by not having any fun, he hired preachers to preach to him about redemption. There was not much else to listen to in those dark days before talk radio. Then one day he experienced a profound spiritual crisis that convinced him he was safely redeemed and did not have to worry about going to hell. Well, he was relieved to get that over with! The crisis turned out to be in his spleen.

Oliver was a born politician. In fact, the surname *Cromwell* may be derived from the old English *crumb,* meaning crooked, although you never heard them mention it. As a Member of Parliament he was conspicuous for his uncouth behavior, even in a parliament not particularly noted for its couthness. As a public speaker he rambled and sermonized like a demented preacher and was not above weeping or throwing cushions to make a point. His "subject matter would not bear much of reason," said Philip Warwick. When he didn't get his way Oliver would throw a tantrum (or a cushion) and threaten to move to America, a vast howling wilderness.

In those days the English could not agree on where to find the ultimate authority, in a monarch, a parliament, a constitution, a republic, etc.[22] Some thought that only Jesus should have authority, but no one knew where to find him. King Charles insisted that his own authority was absolute and God-given, though he

---

[21] Pronounced potpourri.
[22] Now authority is computerized and finds us.

needed Parliament to put up the money. Charles was an autocrat, and rather a brat. Oliver felt that Parliament should be in charge, not the king, as the king had married a Papist and Parliament had not. It was not fair that the king got to make all the important mistakes. But Charles refused to submit to Parliament, instead he raised an army. So did Parliament, and just in time too, for soon there was a civil war going on, to decide whether the people of England should be oppressed by a popish king or by a Presbyterian parliament. People who understand the English civil wars are peculiar. Not being peculiar myself, I cannot help you much. Even the soldiers did not understand them. I doubt that our man Cromwell did. If you could figure out the Presbyterians, you might stand a chance. Well, maybe.

The king started it. Or did he? Anyway, his men were called Cavaliers because the word *Tory* had not yet been invented. Parliament's troops were called Roundheads because of their ridiculous haircuts. There were no good guys. Both sides fought like savage beasts. Roundheads used churches as stables or latrines; Cavaliers preferred to desecrate people.

Oliver stole some horses and formed an army of Roundheads.[23] He trusted in God, kept his powder dry, and usually prevailed in battle because God was on his side. When he won, it proved that God was on his side. When he didn't win, it meant that God wanted him to try harder. He selected his men carefully, to ensure that they were fanatical enough, and disciplined them so well that they butchered their enemies like gentlemen of quality, although they were the sort who in normal times would have been busy filling dung carts. They chanted psalms as they roared into battle, just to remind everyone whose side God was on. In battle, Oliver was "as another man is

---

[23] It is surprising how many great men started out as horse thieves.

when he hath drunken a cup of wine too much," said Richard Baxter.

Oliver believed it was OK to kill people on the Sabbath, as long as it was not fun. So he tried not to enjoy it too much. His partner, the Holy Spirit, also worked weekends. Oliver's personal motto was: "Let peace be sought through war." In fact, Oliver loved peace so much that he was continually at war.

Anyway, Oliver and the Roundheads prevailed in the wars. The king was captured, but Presbyterians in Parliament were still not willing to put him out to pasture. So there was a purge of Presbyterians from the House of Commons. What was left was called "the Rump" or "Fag-end" or "Dreggs," because that's what it was. England became a rumpocracy, ruled by a rump.

Then one day Oliver saw the finger of God reaching down from the sky and darned if it wasn't pointing right at the king! Oliver and his Rumpers decided it was time for King Charles Stuart to be brought to judgment, so his head was chopped off, to teach him a lesson. This is known to history as Oliver's first major blunder. It was also the king's last major lesson. Royalists are still sore about it. But King Charles learned his lesson; he never again tried to hand over England as a present to the pope. He and his head were carried into heaven by angels and behaved themselves admirably after that.

Meanwhile, Ireland was ablaze with rebellion so, in 1649, with the king safely tucked away and Parliament safely purged, Oliver went there to introduce the blessings of English civilization to the Irish, whether they wanted them or not. They wanted food instead, they were starving. Oliver believed that the Irish were priest-ridden, vicious, drunken, miserable, barbarous wretches and not human. He didn't like them much. As a matter of fact, if you give them food, the Irish become more human—about as human as foreigners can ever get.

At Drogheda, his men massacred more than three thousand Irish with blind animal ferocity, but mostly with swords. Oliver said it was the direct work of the Holy Spirit. At Wexford, Oliver wanted to show mercy, but two thousand more Irish were butchered by the righteous hand of the Holy Spirit. Can nothing be done about the Holy Spirit?

Religious persecution followed. Oliver believed in freedom of conscience for all "godly" people, but he would be the judge of who was godly. (Never mind about that time he voted for the execution of the archbishop of Canterbury. Why bring that up?) Liberty of conscience was a great, fundamental human right, he insisted, but Papists, Anglicans, and atheists were not great, fundamental, or human.

Oliver tried to convert the Irish to Protestantism by murdering them, stealing their land, exiling them to Barbados, hunting down their priests, assiduous preaching, driving them "to hell and Connaught"—but mainly by showing them a good example.

Then those pesky Scots invaded England. They wanted everyone to be Presbyterian, so Oliver had to go fight with them too. Presbyterians liked bishops, and Oliver couldn't stand uppity bishops telling him what to do. He always credited God for his victories, even when they became defeats two days later, but, according to royalist sources, Oliver sold his soul to the devil on 3 September 1651, just before the battle of Worcester. He won that battle without God's help, and that finally ended the English civil wars. Give the devil some credit, I guess.

Meanwhile, there was a power vacuum in England. Oliver believed in parliamentary government answerable to the people, but only to the right people. He believed that only property owners should be allowed to vote. Papists disagreed, as their property had been stolen by Oliver and his ancestors. Everyone was tired of taking orders from a rump, as who wouldn't be? So in 1653, Oliver drove the Rumpers out. This was known as "dissolving the Rump" or Oliver's second major blunder.

Dissolving the Rump

Naturally, this did not resolve the power vacuum. They tried a "Parliament of Saints" called the Barebone's Parliament, but that one did not work out either, as the saints could not get along with one another. You know how saints are—impossible to live with. Besides, you really can't have a government named after someone like Praise-God Barebone.[24] Where was the gravitas in that?

---

[24] Praise-God Barebone was a rakish MP, rabble-rousing preacher, leathermonger, and inventor of boudoir fripperies. Also a saint and moral authority.

So, having dissolved practically everything but himself, Oliver decided, why not me? Will I do? He believed in government by the good and the wise, but until such a person could be found, he would have to rule by default. He called himself "lord protector." It was not always easy to tell the difference between a king and a lord protector, mainly because there wasn't any, except that lords protector had not signed the Magna Carta and therefore were not restricted by it. He ruled alone, in regal splendor, much as Charles Stuart had, but he did not marry a Papist.

Oliver's foreign policy was dedicated to spreading godliness around the world and stealing gold from Spanish galleons. He took Jamaica from the Spanish because there were not many Papists there to make trouble. He didn't know that the mosquitos were worse than the Papists. He did not approve of the Anglo-Dutch War because he felt that Protestants should not be killing Protestants when there were so many Papists and Jesuits in need of killing.

In his old age Oliver finally loosened up somewhat. He took up drinking and smoking and decided that bearbaiting and cockfighting were not so bad after all, if they did not "constitute the central object of life." He even went a-hawking, though he found it dangerously close to being fun.

He died during a diabolical storm, on the seventh anniversary of the deal he'd made with the devil. His funeral was the most fun the English had seen in years. You should have seen the parties in Amsterdam! But the Irish were not in the mood for partying. They were still starving, and had Henry Cromwell with them, Oliver's son. It is not easy to party with a Cromwell around.

Oliver was succeeded by his ineffectual son Richard, known to history as "Tumble-Down Dick."[25] True to his name, Dick soon tumbled down and Stuarts retook the

---

[25] He was born to tumble down.

throne. It was fun while it lasted, but the revolution was over. Everything returned to what was then believed to be normal, except that "Merrie Englande" was not merrie anymore.

But wait! We're not finished with Oliver yet. His corpse was dug up and hanged from a gallows at Tyburn. Then his head was cut off, stuck on a pole, and displayed for all to gape at for about twenty years, until it finally blew down in a storm. It is not true that a green apple tree grew over his grave. Why should it? Besides, he has no grave. His head is hidden in a wall somewhere. Hibbert says that Oliver was rehabilitated in the nineteenth century by Thomas Carlyle. It is not easy to rehabilitate a decapitated person.

Oliver Cromwell believed in religious toleration and was willing to kill anyone who didn't. He called himself "the Lord's Poor Worm" and I can't improve on that. People used to say he was the greatest Englishman who ever lived, but that was before the Beatles. A few Jews thought he was the promised messiah, but were talked out of it. To the Irish he was always simply "the Fiend Incarnate."

"He goeth furthest who knows not whither he is going," said Oliver, which explains why he went so far![26] Oliver's life teaches us that if you cut off somebody's head, somebody might cut off yours. Fair is fair, after all. For up-to-date information about Oliver Cromwell, inquire at any Irish pub.

---

[26] Few people know that Oliver Cromwell discovered a cure for pimples. Those who care are even fewer.

Anthony Comstock

Anthony Comstock was a crusader for clothing. He believed that clothing was next to godliness. As a youth in Connecticut he loved going to church, so one wonders why he did not become a clergyman, a man of the cloth. Instead he became a clothing salesman, dedicated to clothing America from head to foot and from coast to coast, especially female Americans. Why do there have to be naked women everywhere you look? he complained. And swearing, why is it everywhere? Why is there a torrent of filth pouring over the land?[27] And Demon Rum? Can't people learn to control themselves?[28]

It is not true that he was born fully clothed. In fact, he was born as naked as a jaybird. But that was in 1844, before he knew any better, before he had any sense of decency. Call it youthful indiscretion. Cut him some slack. He didn't really mean it. You ask, did Tony ever sow wild oats in his youth? Never! He skipped that phase of development entirely.

He was soon to declare war on naked bodies, certain bodily functions, French playing cards, "dirty" pictures, indecent rubber goods, and other "baits of the devil." Also racy books. He read George Eliot, Sir Walter Scott, and the clean parts of the Bible, but not much else. Who needed to read anything else? He regarded pornographers as mad dogs, and they felt much the same about him.

It started out as a hobby. He might have lived his life an obscure dry goods salesman in Brooklyn but for his itch to meddle in the affairs of other people. When he saw offences against what he believed to be decency he notified the authorities. If they did not act promptly enough, he acted himself. He was a doer, not a thinker. If he had thought, how could he have done? He became informer-general to the YMCA, or *rattus vulgaris* in the original Latin.

In 1873 he retired from dry goods to become a full-time vice hound and self-appointed agent of Christ. President Grant appointed him official vice hound of the U.S. mails. By this time Tony had expanded his scope of objections to include contraceptive devices, syringes, medical books, scientific treatises on the propagation of marsupials, the tango and the hoochie-coochie, unclad mannikins, dime novels, nickel novels, flesh and spirit,

---

[27] Connecticut was a wild place in those days.
[28] If you gave him a shot of whiskey, Comstock would pour it onto the ground.

the sportin' life, Turkish abominations, the sheath skirt, pictures in cigar store windows, dancers "who dance without moving their legs," dancers "who bend away back." Sorry, I haven't room to list them all, but you get the idea. He was a busy man. He believed that sex was the filthy side of life and if you just ignored it it would go away. But some people didn't want it to go away. They thought it kind of spiced things up.

Comstock married an older woman who reminded him of his mother. Notable for her taciturnity, Mrs. Comstock was a daughter of a parson. Comstock called her "Wifey." She called him her "dear good boy." A pity that Dr. Freud did not live with them—what a book his notes could have made! Somehow the Comstocks had a daughter, born stark naked, but not for long.[29] They adopted another daughter, who had to be institutionalized. (I'm not saying why; I'm just telling you.)

The Comstocks were always fully overdressed, usually in black. Some historians claim that he wore red flannel underwear, but I can't prove it. According to Heywood Broun, "It is not to be denied." Mrs. Comstock also dressed in black. Comstock probably didn't know himself what color underwear she wore. I'd guess black. What do you think? This would be a good topic for a doctoral thesis.

To hear Tony tell it, lust was public enemy number one, Satan's favorite snare, worse even than Demon Rum. Free lusters were no better than Turks, said Comstock, who could always spot people enslaved by secret sins "that cannot survive the light of day." He could tell by their sunken, lust-crazed eyes, their pallid, vacant, idiotic faces, their hollow cheeks and leprous, wasted, debilitated bodies.

Comstock believed that books could be dangerous. "One cannot get away from a book that has once been read," he warned. By the way, are you sure you want to

---

[29] A virgin birth has been ruled out.

33

continue reading this one? You will not be able to unread it later. Tony believed that the brains of children were composed of highly absorbent spongy matter. Ever try to get a book out a sponge? Comstock said, "Every child should have a Bible of its own." Minus the naughty bits, of course.[30]

In those days, jurors were not allowed to read smutty books before judging them obscene, but Comstock did. It was his duty to read them, especially the seduction scenes. Somebody had to do it! Was it his fault that duty

---

[30] Let us be thankful that Tony did not publish his own version of the Bible. He would have reduced it to a pamphlet.

stationed him in a swamp at the mouth of a sewer? And he loved it! He liked to be where the slime was thickest. He believed that smutty books caused idiocy, madness, epilepsy, etc. After all, look what they did to him! His satchel of pictures of naked women got the attention of congressmen in Washington, who passed a statute called the Comstock Law. It is still on the books as we go to press. It banned "obscenities" from the mails. And who was to decide what an "obscenity" was? Our man Comstock volunteered for the job! He was a world-class authority on what he called "smutt."[31] He knew it when he saw it, even if it wasn't there. He was very broad-minded. No one had a broader idea of what might be considered lewd.

So Tony got to define "public morals" and "common decency" for the rest of us. Like Torquemada of the Spanish Inquisition, he did penance for his sins by punishing others for theirs. But it is not true that he was the world champion book burner of all time because many of the books he seized were not burned at all. They were dumped into the East River where, it should be noted, they caused no discernible increase in vice among the fishes. As Torquemada dumped no books into the East River, he had an advantage in the book burning derby.

Comstock was proud of the books he had destroyed, but refused to mention their names, for fear of creating feverish demand for them. He is credited with blank pages in ancient and modern classics, such as the writings of Zola and Boccaccio, and was responsible, by his own admission, for the destruction of 160 tons of "dirty" literature and pictures. Although not everything he destroyed has been missed, Heywood Broun likened him to a granite rock standing in the way of American art and literature.

---

[31] He never did learn to spell the word.

Tony deplored newspapers. They "oozed corruption from the debauched." They were nothing but "putrid matter" left at our very doors, leaving a stench worse than decaying carrion. As for art, it was OK if it kept its clothes on and didn't parade itself before the eyes of the public.

By driving so many "smutt" dealers out of business, Comstock discovered that he had endangered his own livelihood, and there was competition from Dr. Parkhurst's group. Was there enough "smutt" around to support both groups? Not always. Sometimes he had to turn his energies against other causes: quacks, swindlers, lotteries, church raffles, and various and sundry frauds. He did some creditable work on the fraud front, but when sex was not involved, his heart was not in it. He even had a woman arrested for calling her husband a "spitzbub." (A spitzbub is a close cousin to a rapscallion.)

Comstock boasted of driving fifteen people to suicide, but there were probably others. "The world is better off without them," he said, proudly. But his obstruction of birth control probably resulted in many more people being born, so it was OK. He had miscreants sentenced to almost six hundred years of prison time. If all his victims were laid end to end, they would reach to the infernal regions.

His methods have been criticized. They included espionage, blackmail, forgery, entrapment, deceit, theft, deviousness, violence, etc. He believed it was OK to fight dirty when fighting something dirty. Sometimes it was necessary to "set aside" the law in order to enforce it. He was frequently involved in fights and carried a loaded revolver. But it was a good Christian revolver, the kind Jesus would have carried. He sustained bodily scars and dished them out too, because that's how it was in the purity business.

Comstock was immune to bribery. The Louisiana Lottery offered him a five year European vacation if he would only be "reasonable." Instead he put the lottery out of business. He never cared for Europe anyway; that's where "French protectors" came from. Not to mention those lust-crazed Italians.

Comstock made many enemies in his career of meddling, such as sneering, godless liberals "who print the name of God in small letters." And proprietors of rumholes, or of candy stores that opened on Sundays. Those who opposed him were known as "dirt lovers." But he had fans as well. Cartoonists loved his muttonchop whiskers. He had winsome eyes—if the lighting was not too good. He could look as wistful as Peter Pan if he tried. He was very popular with prudes, prigs, and Puritan fanatics, who shared his moral sense, or lack thereof. He inadvertently promoted the careers of artists such as George Bernard Shaw, "that Irish smutt dealer," by creating controversy about their work. His condemnation was the kind of publicity that could create superstars overnight. I wish he were still around to condemn my books!

Comstock saw himself as a sewer worker, and a happy one. He was a weeder in God's garden, pulling out thorns and thistles dangerous to tender young shoots. Protecting people, even people who did not want to be protected. Others saw him as a sanctimonious fanatic, a puritanical nut case. No longer obscure, his name made it into Webster's Dictionary under *Comstockery*. Tony's definition differed from the one usually accepted: officious meddling.

Comstock's death was brought on by overdoing at a purity convention, as he never did learn to control himself. Too much purity can be exhausting. Most historians agree that he is now in heaven, but very bored there. He still hates the devil, but needs him around to make life interesting. Like rat catchers who need rats to be personally fulfilled, heavenly vice hounds like Comstock need to make regular visits to the "other" place for reasons of personal fulfillment, as St. Peter does not allow "smutt" inside the pearly gates.

To the pure all things are pure, said Tony, who saw lewdness everywhere. But he was not all bad, as he once shot a rabid dog. I could tell you more about him, but have to watch what I say—the Comstock laws are still on the books.

It was a shame that Tony missed his calling. He would have been a darn good dry goods salesman. One of the all-time greats! But it is too late for that now. His life teaches us how obscene censorship can be.

II

Damyanks

Andrew Jackson

U. S. Grant

Woodrow Wilson

William Randolph Hearst

Andrew Jackson

Andrew Jackson was known as "Old Hickory" or "Sharp Knife" or "King Andrew I" or simply "the Jackass," depending upon your point of view. He saw himself as an avenging angel born to drive the British out of North America and into hell. The Brits were the stuff of his nightmares, going back to the scar they gave him during the Revolutionary War in the Carolinas. They stole his childhood and refused to give it back. He would have despised the Beatles even!

For years North and South Carolina have been squabbling over where Jackson was born. As it does not alter the price of peanut butter one cent, it is irrelevant and immaterial. He believed he was born on the South Carolina side of the border and that's good enough for me. After he became a war hero in 1815, Jackson suddenly had more birthplaces than a basketball team. Six or seven birthplaces ought to be enough for anyone!

His pious mother wanted him to become a Presbyterian preacher, but he was a rip-roaring, rollicking fellow, given to fighting, gambling, boozing, wrecking furniture, venting steam, and wenching with wild women.[32] He swore a blue streak and scared people half to death with his blood-curdling oaths. He was not noticeably Christian, other than an occasional Presbyterian expression on his face. Clearly he was not cut out for a pulpit, though he could hate with biblical fury.

Instead he became a frontier lawyer in Tennessee, then believed to be the Wild West. He was paid in salt, coon skins, whiskey, tallow, beeswax, cowbells, bacon, etc. You can't get ahead that way, so he went into real estate, as there was money to be made in selling land that legally belonged to Native Americans, then believed to be Indians.

Presidential from the beginning, he had an indomitable will, though his body was on the domitable side. He had uncivil habits, such as chewing tobacco and spitting while conducting business. He foamed at the mouth when angry and had a tendency to slobber at inopportune times. In short, he was a natural for politics. Being a judge in 1798 was his first real job. Then he joined the military in 1801.

The trouble with Indians was that they were in the way of what was then believed to be progress.[33] Also they were not human, as demonstrated by their aligning with the British. Jackson decided they would be happier in Oklahoma, a place God had created especially for Indians. The Indians disagreed. They liked it fine right where they were, but Jackson removed the Creeks, Cherokees, Choctaws, and Chickasaws to Oklahoma anyway.[34] He

---

[32] Many people have forgotten that Jackson overturned outhouses in his youth.

[33] Mexicans also were in the way, even when they were in Mexico.

[34] This was before oil was discovered in Oklahoma.

paid them fair and square for their land, ten cents per acre. If they wouldn't sell he took it in the so-called Indian wars. He felt he had a right to take it, after they had put him to the considerable expense of evicting them. This was known as frontier justice. Jackson promised the Indians they could live happily ever after in Oklahoma "as long as grass grows or water runs," but neglected to disclose how little grass or water there was there. It is true that he broke some of his promises to the Indians, but remember, he made up for them with new promises. Those too he broke. Indian removal must be "voluntary," he insisted, so intimidation and bribery were used, as needed, to secure the consent of the Indians.

At Horseshoe Bend, Alabama, in 1814 he secured the consent of the Creeks by killing so many of them that he was promoted to brigadier general of the U.S. Army. The bloodbath was necessary, he said, because the Indians refused to be civilized. Afterwards, he cut off their noses, heaped them in a big pile, and counted them. He wanted credit for each and every nose. Then he claimed twenty-three million acres of Indian land, as the Indians did not know what to do with it.

But killing Indians was not nearly as satisfying as killing Brits, and Jackson was itching for payback. He got his chance at New Orleans in 1815. He believed that God intervened at New Orleans. Nevermind that the battle was fought by mistake, fifteen days on the wrong side of the peace treaty at Ghent. You really shouldn't expect God to be up-to-date on Belgium. Belgium, indeed! The English wanted to colonize Louisiana, but Jackson stopped them. Otherwise, the people of that region would be dropping their aitches today.

So Jackson became a war hero and a political force to be reckoned with. President Monroe wanted to make him ambassador to Russia, to get rid of him, but Thomas Jefferson warned that Jackson would start a quarrel with Russia within a month. So instead he was made governor of Florida. There was a quarrel in less than a month. Monroe couldn't stand it when Jackson called him "Jim."

About 1822 Jackson decided to rein in his behavior somewhat because he wanted to run for president. He thought a president should be a tad above average in morality. Shows how much he knew about history! He lost the election in 1824 because of what he called a "corrupt bargain." Some sources say a "dirty deal," although it was not especially dirty—for politics.

The presidential campaign of 1828 *was* especially dirty, even for politics. It was vicious and nasty and sordid, and Jackson won. The validity of his marriage to Rachel Donelson was a hot issue. He claimed he had married her in 1791, but had he really? The legal circumstances were dubious, so they did it again in 1794, just in case it didn't take the first time. By 1794 they should have been legally married, after two tries.

Rachel should have been beyond reproach anyway, as she looked like a short, fat dumpling. "She shows how far the skin can be stretched," quipped a Southern wag.[35] He loved his "Rachael."[36] He thought she was a high-class lady. She wasn't especially, although she smoked only the finest imported "segars." It takes more than high-class "segars" to make a lady. Some complained that she relaxed public morals but, if you ask me, some of the morals in those days needed to be relaxed. Frankly, I don't care whether she was a bigamist or not. Now can we move on?

Jackson had political appeal. He was as ignorant as the voters, and they appreciated that. He appealed to the "common man," as he was so common himself. In fact, he was hardly ever proper. His butchering of Indians and Brits added to his appeal, as did his generosity with his

---

[35] The Jacksons looked like the Jack Sprats, but it is not true that he lived on acorns. Why should he?

[36] John Quincy Adams claimed that Jackson could not spell his own name. He could so, but not Rachel's.

whiskey. Soon he was more popular than Washington, Jefferson, Franklin, and Jesus combined. But many favored Jackson as vice president, a position from which he could hang nobody. Tocqueville said, "All the enlightened classes are opposed to General Jackson." But enlightened people, as usual, were outnumbered by ignorant boobs.

A genius at the art of unproductive controversy, Jackson was forever dueling over his wife's so-called honor, an issue that has not been resolved as we go to press. But it is not true that he was so full of lead that he rattled when he walked. There were only two bullets lodged in his body, and they didn't rattle at all. You'd hardly know they were there. It was his bones that rattled. Dueling was his way of establishing the proper pecking order. "My reputation is dearer to me than life," he said, forgetting how little use reputation is to a dead man. It didn't take much to set him off. Just call him "a coward and a poltroon" or use Rachel's sacred name in vain and his impulse management skills would snap, resulting in yet another "affair of honor" at dawn, just over the state line, with pistols.[37] He could not seem to handle that word *poltroon*. It pushed his buttons. Dueling was not very effective. After all his "affairs of honor," Jackson's honor remained about the same. Hers too. He preferred to duel only prominent people, such as "Nolichucky Jack," the governor of Tennessee, but gave up dueling in 1822, when he became a candidate for the presidency. There were already enough complaints about his so-called character. One of his dueling foes had had the effrontery to die of his wounds.

Jackson was vague on political issues, except those involving the British or his wife's honor. According to Professor Abernethy, no historian has ever accused Jackson of having a political philosophy or any political principles. He was a man of the people, but of the wrong people. An opportunist, in time he came to be called a Democrat or a Slavocrat. He believed in "plain" government, even homely government, but was partisan enough to merit his very own opposition party. The Whig Party was created mainly to keep an eye on him.

Upon becoming president, Jackson's first item of business was "Operation Clean Sweep," a general housecleaning, to scrape the barnacles from the ship of state, to clean the "Augean stables" of government corruption. He turned hundreds of scamps and rascals out of government jobs and replaced them with more congenial, more Jacksonian, rogues. Jackson believed

---

[37] In writing a challenge to a duel, Jackson used the complimentary close, "your obedient servant." Can you think of one more appropriate under the circumstances?

that simpleminded rustics could do government jobs just fine, as long as they were good-hearted, hated the British, and had no opinions about Rachel. Competence would be nice, of course, but he had never found it to be necessary. Alas, sharpies bamboozled millions from his government.

The "Petticoat War" flared up in 1829. This concerned whether Peggy Eaton, wife of Jackson's secretary of war, was a slut. The government became polarized into two camps: those who snubbed Mrs. Eaton as a slut and those who did not. There was no in-between. Jackson defended Mrs. Eaton because she reminded him of Rachel.[38]

Jackson accomplished much in his two terms as president:

* He rid the White House of bed bugs and all traces of John Quincy Adams.
* He ended the Era of Good Feeling.
* He gave the Democratic Party its symbol, the jackass.
* He paid off the national debt, though he could not pay off his own debts.
* He pushed more Indians west, where they would be happier.
* He rattled sabers and collected war indemnities.
* He caught hell for the Panic of 1837 and the depression that followed it.

Jackson was the first U.S. president to appoint someone to office who subsequently stole a million dollars from the government. Also the first to ride a train, to smoke a corn cob pipe, to be given a fourteen hundred pound cheese.[39] He got his picture on the twenty dollar bill. If you think that is easily done, try it yourself

---

[38] Personally, I have no opinion about Mrs. Eaton. I'd rather not get involved.

[39] The cheesy smell lingered in the White House into the Van Buren administration.

sometime. It was especially difficult for him, as he was against paper money.

Jackson had only two regrets about his two terms in office: that he had not shot Henry Clay or hanged John C. Calhoun. There's always something. He retired to his estate near Nashville, Tennessee, called the Hermitage, where he dealt in cotton, horses, tobacco, swan skins, slaves, and other commodities. He made money from stud fees, but couldn't get ahead because his adopted son was forever signing things that he shouldn't have been signing. Hickory canes became the rage, especially those cut at the Hermitage. They were the hula hoops of their day. Jackson could have made a fortune from spin-offs, but had no business sense.

Jackson owned more than 150 slaves. He claimed they were contented, but they often voted with their feet. He never whipped them, unless they deserved it. He didn't like lashing women and children, so used a smaller switch on them. He seldom gave females more than forty lashes, and then only when they needed them. He cared about the health and condition of his slaves, almost as much as he cared about his race horses. Some of his slaves even had shoes! On one occasion he called the white folks' doctor to see an injured slave child, fearing she would become a cripple. He didn't like crippled slaves. Jackson became so dependent upon his slaves that he wanted them to join him in heaven, even those he had sold in New Orleans. At least in heaven his slaves would not be forever running away.

It is said that when Jackson died at the Hermitage in 1845, his pet parrot was so overcome with grief that it had to be removed from the funeral for swearing. You have to admire someone who can inspire that kind of devotion.

Jackson gave us the Age of Jackson, Jacksonville, and Jackson Day dinners. Joseph Smith said that the Garden of Eden was in Jackson County, Missouri, but Adam and Eve had no way of knowing that at the time. "Jacksonian democracy" looked good on paper, but never actually existed for most people, even most white people. Democracy is much like the Easter bunny, all warm and fuzzy, but not really there. He pretended to be a populist hero, the people's friend, but his private letters tell a different story. He deserves some credit for killing the big, bad, Bank of the United States. Hooray!

Keep in mind that Jackson did not invent violence. I forget who did. Probably Cain. His life teaches us that any inarticulate boob can be president. But we already knew that, didn't we?

U. S. Grant

In his youth, Ulysses Grant was known as "Useless Grant." He was considered a numbskull with no sense. But animals liked him, especially horses, as he lacked the normal boyhood propensity for killing and torturing animals.

His father tanned hides for a living and wanted his son to do the same, but Ulysses did not like bloody hides. They were messy, and besides, he did not approve of killing animals. Animals were his pets, his best friends. They understood him. He did not care about people, however, so his father sent him off to West Point to learn how to kill people. But mainly to get an education at government expense.

Grant was bored at West Point. Not interested in a military career, he did not want to be there. He wanted to read romantic novels, not lessons, but somehow managed to graduate. He would have been first in his French class, he said, "if the class had been turned the other end foremost." Meanwhile he cultivated his inborn talent for being unnoticeable, and majored in horsemanship.

Grant did not approve of the Mexican War, believing it to be rapacious and unjust, but enlisted in it anyway, because duty required him to be rapacious and unjust. He fought on the same side as Jeff Davis and Robert E. Lee— there were no good guys. "We were sent to provoke a fight," he said; a job was a job.

Assigned to the Pacific Northwest, Grant tried to make money shipping ice to San Francisco; it melted. He planted potatoes and oats, but lost them to floods. He bought up all the chickens near Fort Vancouver; they died. He opened a billiards club in San Francisco; his partner absconded with the money. Such was his business acumen. At Fort Humboldt, threatened with court martial because of his drinking, he "resigned" his commission and drifted back to Missouri, "poor and forlorn."

In Missouri, the pattern continued. He failed as a farmer, firewood dealer, store clerk, hack driver, rental agent, historical personage, etc.[40] He called his farm "Hardscrabble" because it did not pay, even with slave labor! By 1858 "Hardscrabble Sam" was a confirmed failure in life, with **DEFEAT** written all over his face in Bodoni Bold. The man was a downer, the sort you would cross the street to avoid meeting. He would have sold his chance to be president for a shot of whiskey. The odds against his ending up on the fifty dollar bill were out of this world. By 1860, stooped and ragged with failure, he hit bottom with a dull thud.

---

[40] Grant failed as an actress while stationed in Texas. He played a very unconvincing Desdemona in Shakespeare's *Othello*.

Although not born poor, Grant had managed to achieve poverty. But he was ambitious. He wanted more from life than forty acres and a mule. He wanted adulation, whiskey, fast horses, horse-faced women, Boston baked beans, cigars. Woodward says he was by nature a drifter: "He had drifted into West Point, drifted into the army, drifted out of it, drifted in and out of dozens of hopeless occupations." Wherever would he drift next? He drifted to Galena, Illinois, where he found that he had only one thing in common with the locals: like them, he wanted to get the hell out.

Then came the Civil War, an equal opportunity employer. The dawn of a new day! Given a brigade, Grant made a success of it for three reasons:

    * He had an inability to surrender, no matter how hard he tried.[41]

    * He had a low and gross conception of war.

    * Cigars. He was unflappable with a cigar in his mouth.

Grant liked to smoke cigars during battle. It was his way of dealing with his nerves. When in crisis he would light up and press on. And it usually worked! His children collected empty cigar boxes as war trophies. People sent him more cigars than he could give away, so he smoked them.

Grant did not like soldiering. Army life had little to recommend it. It meant feasting on mule meat, cornbread, hardtack. (Civil War hardtack was hard enough to stop a bullet.) It was no fun smoking cigars in the rain. Besides, he sickened at the sight of blood, even other people's blood. War was foolish, brutal, and unnecessary, he believed, but duty required him to be foolish and brutal in order to make himself necessary.

So in 1861 Grant drove the rebels out of their camp at Belmont, Missouri. They soon returned. Fort Henry

---

[41] The "F" word (failure) terrified him more than the enemy did.

surrendered before Grant arrived. At Fort Donelson he was alleged to be drunk but nevertheless demanded "unconditional surrender" of General Buckner, who thought the terms unchivalrous, as he had once bailed out Grant when he was down and out. Caught by surprise at Shiloh, Grant would have been driven out of the history books and into hell if Buell had not arrived. He was off to an unpromising start.

Vicksburg was a Pyrrhic victory because a careless servant emptied Grant's washbowl, with his false teeth in it, into the Mississippi River. So no more hardtack for a while. Grant got credit for driving the rebels away from Chattanooga, but admitted that he had nothing to do with it. The Battle of the Wilderness was a pointless bloodbath within a pointless bloodbath. Cold Harbor was so hopeless from the start that Grant apologized for it in his memoirs. Petersburg was a cat fight and the Battle of the Crater a complete fiasco. Grant's military strategy was flawed but worked, mainly because he had the biggest army in the world.[42] He came to be known as "the Butcher," but Lincoln did not object to the butcher's bill. Those who paid the bill were too dead to complain.

In any case, the South finally cried "uncle" and Grant got credit for "winning" the war, as if such a disaster could ever be won. The Grim Reaper was the real winner, and the vultures. But after Vicksburg Grant smelled of victory, an aroma powerful enough to mask the smell of wholesale carnage. After Chattanooga, Grant was more popular than Lincoln, until Lincoln took back the lead by being murdered. How could Grant trump that one? On that fateful day in April 1865, the Grants had been invited to Ford's Theater by the Lincolns. But that awful Mrs. Lincoln would be there, so the Grants made other plans.

---

[42] Grant won the war of attrition by a score of 243-190 (in thousands of deaths).

Grant's wife was a horse-faced woman, Julia Dent, said to be a "regular little brick."[43] Grant called her "Dado," but most people knew her as "the Boss." She didn't like the Civil War, believing that the South had a right to go out of the Union if it wanted to.[44] "All the comforts of slavery passed away forever," she moaned. "We had such fine old servants at home that I was under the impression that the house kept itself." The war was about slavery, said Grant; then why did Julia bring a slave to wait on her when she visited her general at the front? Wasn't she missing the point? Grant had no strong views about slavery, but thought "thinking people" should be in charge. Thinking people meant white people with property. Grant was white, but no amount of property could have made him a thinking person.

---

[43] But Gore Vidal called her "a goose of a wife."
[44] After the war, Julia was chummy with Varina Davis, the wife of Jefferson Davis.

Grant's father-in-law, "Colonel" Dent, was an unreconstructed Southerner who haunted the White House when Grant was president, mixing mint juleps, smoking cigars, and complaining about damned Yankees and upstart "niggahs." No wonder blacks kept their distance from the White House! Grant's father also kept his distance from "Colonel" Dent, as who wouldn't? The last slave-owning president, Grant was torn between his abolitionist father and his slave-owning wife, who refused to give up her slaves until forced by law to do so. He wanted to annex Santo Domingo, in the Caribbean, as a dumping ground for freed slaves.

Grant did not mind Native Americans if they lived in houses, wore trousers, and voted Republican, especially those who called him "the Great White Father." The trouble with Indians was that they were like Grant—never satisfied with forty acres and a mule. But Grant felt that they should not be annihilated, and some of them returned the sentiment.

President Johnson tried to send Grant to Mexico to get rid of him, but he refused to go. Finally Grant was made president, as he had failed at so many other occupations. What else can you do with such people? He did not want to be president but, as usual, drifted into it. The poor man needed a job! He was an attractive candidate because he had no ideas of his own that anyone could object to. He was the most silent president until Coolidge. What was there to say? "Let us have peace," was his campaign slogan. Who could argue with that? At least it was better than his war slogan: "I propose to move immediately[45] upon your works."

Grant's administration featured continued drift. It became so corrupt that it split into regulars, who liked corruption as it was, and mugwumps, who wanted to improve it. The regulars had to split again, into stalwarts and halfbreeds. Grant aligned with the stalwarts, who

---

[45] Pronounced immejetly.

believed that the corruption they had was already good enough and didn't need reforming. Corruption became the national pastime, as night baseball was not yet available. Grant was accused of nepotism, but in fact he gave only twelve jobs to his relatives. No, I don't know how many relatives he had. He regarded the presidency as a trophy, not a job. How was he to know that he was expected to do things?

The highlights of Grant's presidency were mostly lowlights. They included scandals of epic proportions, Black Friday, the Panic of '73, hard times, the Whiskey Ring, the salary grab of '73,[46] Custer's last stand, coal strikes, moral ebbtide, the collapse of Reconstruction, etc. Sorry, but I don't have space to list all the outrages. No wonder the seventies was known as "the Dreadful Decade." Historians disagree on which of Grant's two terms was more dreadful. I'd say the second, because the Panic of '73 lasted until '79. But the invention of barbed wire was not his fault.

Politics was too rough for Grant, who was out of his element. Woodward says, "his administration was a vast, smoky confusion." But the corruption wasn't his fault, as he didn't know what was going on. What could he do? He was only the president! Secretary of War John Rawlins was the brains behind Grant. His death in 1869 left Grant completely brainless.[47]

Grant drifted out of the presidency, as quietly as he had drifted in, and became a wandering UFP (unattached famous personage). Having had enough of America, he ran away from home for two years on a round-the-world trip. "Venice would be a fine place if it were drained," he opined. He was treated like royalty by Europeans, who had not been inconvenienced much by his bloodbath, but

---

[46] The salary grab doubled Grant's salary, retroactive to 1871, while he was vetoing pensions for other people.
[47] General McClernand also complained of "furnishing brains for Grant."

Victor Hugo refused to meet him. Queen Victoria thought Julia had "funny American ways." The queen was not easily amused.

Back in America, Grant became a fat and puffy Wall Street bourgeois. Mostly he smoked cigars in his office at the Mexican-Southern Railway. In time he lost all his money to a swindler and was back to normal.

There has been much loose talk about Grant's drinking, known in the vernacular as "taking ill." A little whiskey went a long way with him. According to a comrade at Fort Vancouver, "One glass would show on him, and two or three would make him stupid." His drinking made him vulnerable to his enemies, as Democrats accused him of not paying for his drinks.

Grant admitted to drinking on occasion, but not on duty. He called himself "sober as a deacon," but did not specify which deacon. Some called him a "one bottle man," others a "two bottle man." He was "a four-fingered drinker," whatever that was. How many ways are there to drink whiskey? Some say he may have been drinking when he fell off his horse after Vicksburg. Who can say? Grant fell off the wagon more than he fell off horses, but he was a multi-tasker who could do both on the same afternoon.

Grant was parsimonious with emotion, as if he feared he would run out. He never cursed or uttered an oath stronger than maybe "fudge!" or "confound it." His best friends were horses and his personality came to resemble that of a horse. It was said that Mark Twain once made Grant laugh. What a pity that no one caught it on film! Grant was Tom Sawyer all grown up, thought Mr. Twain.

Some thought his thinking rigid but others denied this, arguing that he didn't think at all. He was "pre-intellectual," said Henry Adams, who thought Grant a cave man. His greatest talent was being unnoticeable and, after Vicksburg, even that talent left him. It is not true that Grant disproved evolution because it made a comeback after him.

Grant is mainly remembered for his corruption and his butchery, and his beating the odds onto the fifty dollar bill. But he inspired the largest barbecue in the history of Seattle, Washington, and a new sidewalk in Galena, Illinois. He was the first president to publish a book. Also the first president to be buried in Grant's Tomb. Mark Twain summed him up best when he said that Grant was stranded in a world that did not make sense. Indeed, aren't we all?

Grant's life teaches us to work hard and take charge of our lives, lest we drift into the presidency.

Woodrow Wilson

Woodrow Wilson was president during "the war to end all wars." It did no such thing. Instead it became part one of a series. It was peculiar how he got to be president in the first place, as eggheads like him were not in great demand in Washington.[48] Voters prefer simple-minded presidents because they are more representative. But Wilson ate hot dogs with the right people and the Bull Moose Party split the opposition for him, creating a nice little gap for him to slip through.[49]

He called his program "the New Freedom," which sounded good on paper. But in the real world it brought

---

[48] To make matters worse, Wilson looked like Ichabod Crane.
[49] It was not easy to find a gap around Taft.

military conscription, new taxes, central banking, inflation, big government, witch hunts, slacker raids, J. Edgar Hoover, police state legislation like the Espionage Act and the Sedition Bill, book burnings, liberty cabbage, censorship of the mails, suspension of the Bill of Rights for the duration, restrictions on music by Huns such as Beethoven, wholesale carnage, mud and cooties, gasless Sundays, heatless Mondays, meatless Tuesdays, porkless Thursdays, wartime restrictions on beer production, etc.[50] *Freedom* had a different meaning in those days. By the way, what was wrong with the *old* freedom?

Wilson knew nothing about foreign affairs so always conferred with his secretary of state, William Jennings Bryan, who knew even less. They invaded Cuba, Haiti, the Dominican Republic, Nicaragua, Panama, even Russia. It got to be a bad habit with them. It was Wilson who created the need for FDR's "Good Neighbor Policy."

He didn't know what to do about Mexico, so he invaded it too—repeatedly. It did no good, so he tried "watchful waiting." That didn't work either. He tried practically everything but *Yanqui go home,* to no avail. Wilson sent the navy to seize Veracruz because the Mexicans refused to salute the U.S. flag. After dozens of people had been killed, they still refused, so he had to make do without the salute. He sent the army deep into Mexico after that pesky *banditto* Pancho Villa, who got away. It almost started a war with Mexico but Wilson figured, why bother? There was already a war going on in Europe. No need for another one.

When World War I broke out in Europe in 1914, Wilson insisted that America be strictly neutral. He was so neutral that he hardly ever mentioned that his mother had been born in England or that the Brits were "fighting

---

[50] But don't blame Wilson for Prohibition; he thought near beer was just fine. Not a dry or a wet, Wilson was a moist or a damp.

our fight." In 1915 he decided to enter the war but didn't let on about it, as there was an election coming up.

"The right is more precious than peace," said Wilson, after winning the 1916 election as the *peace candidate*. It wasn't the only thing that was. The war, he said, was to make the world safe for democracy. *Democracy* had the same meaning then as now—it meant bottom line. He believed that the way to end all wars was to have a good one and get it over with.[51] For this he won a Nobel Peace Prize, a remarkable achievement for the commander-in-chief of an enormous military machine during the bloodiest war the world had ever seen! He decided that America must have the biggest navy in the world, but there must be no militarism about it.

At first the British thought Wilson a dud; in the trenches, shells that failed to explode were known as "Wilsons." Allies thought he was yellow, but he showed them! After the U.S. entered the war he was absolutely fearless about sending other people to the front lines.

Military conscription was unpopular with some Americans, but Wilson insisted it was OK because the nation had already volunteered in mass. Or had it? Slackers did not agree that they had volunteered, in mass or otherwise. Slackers were people who didn't fancy being blown to bits for the Yankee dollar, or blowing other people to bits. Or Irish-Americans who didn't want to fight for their British tormenters. Or German-Americans who didn't want to shoot their kinfolk.[52] More than a thousand people were convicted of felonious slacking in the first degree, including a presidential candidate, Eugene V. Debs, a labor leader who was sent to prison. Debs holds the record for presidential votes for a convict: nine hundred thousand. Wilson thought these were too

---

[51] Would you buy a used war from this man? Wilson disapproved of violence, but sometimes threatened to "spankdoodle" his children.
[52] Wilson despised hyphenated Americans.

many votes for a slacker. Those two just couldn't get along. Even after the war ended Wilson refused to pardon Debs, but Debs, still in his prison cell, graciously offered to pardon Wilson.

During his second term as president, Wilson took ill and his wife Edith and his doctor had to rule the country for him. She was the first female president. He became so paranoid that some people thought he was insane, which was only partly true.[53] He did like to surround himself with other paranoid people, such as Mitchell Palmer, his attorney general, who was having a hysterical time rounding up slackers and deporting foreigners by the boatload. And Palmer's young apprentice, J. Edgar Hoover, was showing promise of future mayhem. But the bars on the White House windows were not intended for Wilson. They had been installed during a previous administration.

Wilson was the stiffest president in U.S. history, at least between Jackson and Coolidge. But no one ever called him uptight because the word had not yet been invented. He believed himself to be a moral agent of God Almighty and pastor to the human race.[54] His decisions were made by God, he insisted, and once made, Wilson's mind snapped shut and became impervious to further discussion. Questions of principle do not admit of compromise, he insisted. The problem was that all his decisions were matters of principle.

It was said that he lacked human warmth, but he often got heartburn. Preoccupied with his digestion, he complained that he could not run both his stomach and the government at the same time. William Allen White said that shaking hands with Wilson was like "seizing a

---

[53] Bullitt concluded that Wilson had fourteen nervous breakdowns, but fell short of full-blown lunacy.
[54] Italians built altars to Wilson and lit candles to his portraits. H. L. Mencken said that Wilson was in line for the next vacancy in the Trinity.

ten-cent pickled mackerel."[55] "I can't effervesce in the face of responsibility," said Wilson, who hardly ever effervesced anyway. But he was not as cool as Coolidge.

Wilson created a new federal banking system. His personal finances, however, were done by his wife, as he was no good with numbers. Tumulty, his secretary, said that Wilson's economic reforms ended for all time the possibility of financial panic. And they did too, until the

---

[55] Wilson said he had a "volcano" inside him, but it was mostly dormant.

crash of 1929. Wilson urged U.S. bankers to go to the aid of bankrupt Latin America, forgetting who had bankrupted it in the first place. But Wilson preferred not to get involved, as he was already involved with his stomach.

Some have called Wilson a bigot, but he loved to tolerate people. He could tolerate Jews, if they were not "junkshop Jews." He could tolerate Native Americans if they were Presbyterians or Episcopalians. He could even tolerate Catholics, unless they were what he called "rank Papists." His secretary was a Catholic, but not a "rank Papist." Wilson could tolerate black people if they stayed in their own place with their own kind, where they would be happier. Never mind about the "darky" stories he liked to tell. After all, didn't he send his daughters to school in the South so they could learn to speak "educated nigger"? Lynchings in the South were epidemic during the Wilson years—one about every six days—but "not the business of the federal government." He could tolerate Japanese people too, even when they embarrassed him by insisting that racial equality be written into the covenant of the League of Nations. They were given a piece of Chinese territory to shut them up. Wilson could tolerate racial equality, within reason, but some races were more equal than others.

Wilson could tolerate women too, though he felt that matriarchy was abnormal and sometimes got indigestion when he heard women speak in public. He disliked teaching female students at Bryn Mawr. Why teach them government, he argued, when they could neither vote nor run for public office? Besides, he was not much good at girl talk. But what especially annoyed him was the solemnity with which they wrote his jokes in their notebooks. When frustrated with the Senate, he dismissed it as "a lot of old women." But don't think Wilson didn't like women. He liked his mother, who was a woman; so were both his wives. Wilson had an Oedipal complex, said Dr. Freud; it wasn't fair to call him "the

Human Icicle." Wilson even helped women get the right to vote, after his wife promised they would vote for him.

Wilson was homely to look at, even for a president. He thought he looked like a horse.[56] Is this why he is not on Mount Rushmore? His second wife said he was a "noticeable man."[57] She called him "the skinny man on the horse." Or was it the skinny man who looked like a horse? Theodore Roosevelt said Wilson looked "like the apothecary's clerk." Wilson had a jutting granite jaw as oversized as his vocabulary—Dos Passos called it a "lantern jaw." He could pull his cheeks out like stretched rubber and snap them; luckily he never did it in public. In 1913 a complete record of his facial expression was recorded on motion picture film and sealed inside a pyramid in Egypt. It is still there. Wilson's face somehow got itself onto the $100,000 bill; don't ask me how I know. But enough about the poor man's face! Could he help it?

He was a brilliant public speaker so it was a shame that no one could understand what he was saying. Grover Cleveland on listening to Wilson: "Sounds good. I wonder what it means." According to Walworth, Wilson had a vocabulary of sixty-two thousand words. It must have been tedious to count them! But he used mostly "greasy and meaningless words," said Mencken. Wilson seldom used foul language, except when playing golf or conferring with Secretary of State Bryan.

Wilson might have been tolerable on his own, but got in with the wrong crowd on Wall Street. He used to say that his mind was "open and to let." No wonder the Money Trust moved in and made itself at home! "He could turn off his mind at will," said his daughter Eleanor. Sometimes he would forget to turn it back on.

Wilson was known as "the Magnificent Failure" because he could not get his own country to join the

---

[56] This is not so bad, as many women like horses.
[57] So was Dr. Frankenstein's creature.

League of Nations. Eugene Debs called him "the most pathetic figure in the world." I won't mention what Wilson called Debs. Why bring that up? Wilson believed that his "Fourteen Points" would bring peace to Europe, where God's Ten Commandments had failed so miserably.

Wilson had the best of intentions. Could he help it that forty years of progress slipped into reverse on his watch? He was the last nice man to be elected president; also the first. Humanitarian in the abstract, he had problems with real people, as don't we all? For years he carried a horse chestnut in his pocket for good luck, but it didn't help much. It was probably out of order.

In 1924 Wilson died and went to heaven, where he became the patron saint of Presbyterian dyspeptics. St. Woodrow has been blamed for practically everything from death to taxes, but he didn't really mean it. Was it his fault that the Versailles Treaty led to the rise of Hitler? He didn't even know the man! And how was he to know that his invasion of Soviet Russia would start a cold war? His Creel Commission gave us new and improved models for propaganda and political hysteria, even though we didn't need them.

Some people think Wilson was a great man. If it makes them feel better, I guess there is no harm in it. He had a vision of the New Jerusalem; was it his fault that it turned out like New Jersey? He was the first modern president who danced jigs. There was even a tango named after him: one step forward, two steps back, side step, hesitate. His town drunk impersonation was hilarious.

Wilson's life teaches us that scrambled eggheads don't know it all.

William Randolph Hearst

William Randolph Hearst was the yellowest of the yellow journalists. He believed that journalism should be fun, like Vaudeville and Coney Island, so he offered fun features: color comics, contests and prizes, gossip, glamour and glitz, sex murders, cheesecake, sob sisters, and advice to the lovelorn. "Crime and underwear" was his winning formula.

He was accused of stealing news from rival papers but didn't really need to, as he was good at making up news.[58] This was known as "creative journalism" or "scooping the competition." The news that really happened was boring and available to practically

---

[58] He stole only one side of the news.

everybody, so he improved on it. Anyway, his fun features left little room for news.

But Hearst journalism, if you can call it that, was hard to ignore. A. J. Pegler likened it to "a screaming woman running down the street with her throat cut." Make that a screaming woman in her undies. Hearst reporters haunted city morgues—that was where the action was. Journalism was successful, Hearst believed, when readers responded to it by exclaiming, "Gee-whiz!" This was known as the gee-whiz test. He wanted stupefying headlines every day, even when nothing particularly stupefying was happening.

Appealing to what he called "the rising degeneration," his journals were so moronic that they soon had enormous circulations; his competitors had to abandon their more ignorant readers to him. But businesses were reluctant to advertise in Hearst papers, claiming that his patrons were ignorant boobs who could not read. In 1919 the *New York Daily News* decided to outhearst Hearst by being even more moronic than he was. It worked, and Hearst had to eat humble pie in New York.

You ask, did Hearst create the vulgarity or was it already there in the first place? Did he debauch journalism, or was he only a good judge of an already debauched public taste? It was a bit of both. No doubt he gave the public what it wanted: a bath of bilge from the sewers of life. But a scoop was a scoop, after all, even if it was slime. He sought God, gold, glory, and circulation—mostly circulation. Quality was no substitute for quantity, so he refused to wash his dirty sheet.

The Hearst Credo:
* Don't offend the lumpen majority. It hurts circulation.
* Don't forever scold, carp, or whine. Leave that to the editorial page.
* Never talk when you can scream.
* Entertainment trumps mere news.
* Try to keep typos down to one per sentence.

* Better to be yellow than red.
* Better to be phony than dull.
* Try to make readers recoil in shock.

As a child, "Billy Buster" Hearst was an early prototype of the Katzenjammer Kids. When he was bad he was horrid. He was the type who put tacks on people's chairs. Born into a mining fortune, he saw no need to grow up. At Harvard he majored in practical jokes. At Boston theaters he enjoyed pelting chorus girls with custard pies. Getting his pet alligator drunk was always good for a laugh. In time poor "Charlie" succumbed to alcoholism. Hearst had it stuffed and mounted on his wall, as there were no twelve-step programs for alligators.

Taking over the family paper in San Francisco, "Sausalito Bill" was bursting at the seams with energy, enthusiasm, and journalistic pranks, which followed logically from his pranks at Harvard. He had great fun in San Francisco, but decided to expand to New York, where he looted Joseph Pulitzer's *World* of practically everything and everybody. Even Pulitzer's office cat defected to Hearst's *Journal*. Hearst kidnapped Outcault's comic *Yellow Kid from Hogan's Alley*, but was never charged with kidnapping.

Contrary to popular rumor, Hearst did not start the Spanish-American War or murder President McKinley. Not by himself anyway.

Hearst's journalism overlapped into politics and he wanted to be president. Why not? He had the money. His vast circulation gave him enormous political power and his readers could vote, even if they could not think. So, pretending to be the people's friend, he favored the eight-hour day for workers, except those who worked for him. He supported assistance to the poor, if it was cheaper than justice. He came out for the flag, a full dinner pail, and God Almighty. He feigned populism because that was where the circulation was. His politics always followed his worship of the great god circulation. He was even called an anarchist lunatic, though he was not an anarchist. But

Hearst could not win elections, nor could the losers he backed: Champ Clark, Landon, Willkie, Dewey, MacArthur. Was there a reason why he backed losers? Was it his support that caused them to lose? When he came to be known as William Also-Ran-Dolph Hearst, he finally gave up politics. He just didn't like losing. He should have quit during the presidential campaign of 1902, before his fireworks display killed a dozen spectators.

Hearst would have been the kind of president America deserved, quipped Ambrose Bierce. The first president with a squeaky soprano voice and stage fright. Bierce said that Hearst cooed, that his voice was like "the fragrance of violets made audible." It was not what voters were looking for. Hearst was not an inspired speaker on the campaign trail. "Nothing came out because there was nothing inside," said the *Chicago Record-Herald*. And he had the world's flabbiest handshake, said his cousin. "He just took your hand and dropped it." This would never do in a president! Nor would his unnerving bug-eyed gaze.

Much vilified during World War I for his pro-German sympathies, "Wilhelm Hearst the Hun," was said to be too yellow to be red, white, or blue. He thought Germans were just folks, not brutes. To some, keeping the home fires burning during the war meant burning Hearst newspapers.

But by the 1920s he was in his prime, having reached the full flowering of his mediocrity. The *New York Evening Post* said that Hearst had "slender intellectual equipment," but who needed brains? Didn't he have enough money to buy brains and surround himself with loyal overachievers? Ambrose Bierce, one of his hired brains, called himself "Hearst's chained bulldog."

In 1930, when German Nazis were facing bankruptcy, Hearst bailed them out by paying Hitler for articles. In 1934, Hitler promised Hearst that he would be nice to Jews, and Hearst believed him. He thought Hitler had an honest face, so he paid him handsomely for his propaganda pieces.[59] Hitler was anti-communist and Hearst felt that communism had to be stopped or it would lead to a fascist backlash in America. He feared fascism so much that he became fascist himself. In time he developed vision so acute that he could see Communists and Bolsheviks that weren't even there. His ballyhoo about Communism didn't fool intelligent people, but intelligent people were as rare then as they are today. He was especially wary of the Japanese. "The Yellow Menace," he called them, unaware that many people regarded him as the Yellow Menace.

---

[59] Hitler was often late with his articles. He was busy with other things.

A man of many names, Hearst was known to show girls as "the Wolf." To his wife he was "the Old Scoundrel." Actress Ilka Chase called him "the Octopus," claiming that he goosed her in the swimming pool. Journalists knew him as "Gush" or "the Wizard of Ooze" or "the Mad Hatter of Yellow Journalism" or "the Yellow Fellow." To Al Smith he was "a cuttlefish who emits this black vapor of ink." Westbrook Pegler called him a "gents' room journalist." Orson Welles called him "Charles Foster Kane." To organized labor he was simply "Public Enemy Number One."

Although his mediocrity is legendary, Hearst was not without talent. He could tap dance and yodel beautifully, and turn newspaper pages with his toes. "He made scrambled eggs wonderfully," said his playmate, actress Marion Davies. An authority on chorus girls, he was a master at the art of ogling and even had an honorary doctorate from Oglethorpe University.[60] A splendid horseman, he was an impressive sight on a merry-go-round.

He liked the sales tax, circulation, dachshunds, merry-go-rounds, dodgem cars, fireworks, rockets and whizbangs, clam chowder, baked beans, and codfish. He disliked canned charity, the French, the Japanese, parlor pinks, income taxes, the New Deal, Boss Murphy, stewed pears, and the two thousand people on his enemies list. He disliked "sap-headed college boys," although he often behaved like one. He was against trusts until he became one. Deep down, he was a simple man, content to live on fifteen million dollars a year.

It has been said that Hearst terrorized newsboys and hired gangsters and plug-uglies, that he distorted the news and destroyed democracy, but he was not all bad, as he sometimes supported the right causes for the wrong reasons. How could he be all bad when he was banished from France, expelled from the best schools, hanged in

---

[60] He had a walking stick that whistled at pretty women.

effigy, and damned by three U.S. presidents? Wasn't he against immorality, at least in others? In 1934 he came out against decadence. And don't forget, he gave us Barney Google, Krazy Kat, Happy Hooligan, the Yellow Kid from Hogan's Alley, and countless other indispensable Americans. Mickey Mouse invited Hearst to his twentieth birthday party. What does *that* tell you?

Hearst discovered that there was money in motion pictures, but it was mostly his own money and he never got it back. His business interests included radio, theater, newsreels, mining, ranching, canning, real estate, bribery, blackmail, jingoism, and practically everything else. He even wrote poetry, although one of his poems cost him two hundred thousand dollars in libel awards and court costs. It was probably the most expensive poem ever written. A compulsive shopper, he was forever buying newspapers, castles, politicians, to the limits of his credit and beyond. A notorious art accumulator, he was a pushover for mawkish madonnas. Buy American, he insisted, as he looted Europe of its art, from the awesome to the awful. He believed that a penny borrowed was a penny earned. "My disposition is to expand," he explained. Indeed, in his later years, Hearst came to resemble a pear.

By 1929 he owned twenty-eight newspapers, if you can call them newspapers, all with boob-catching headlines, front-page editorials, pseudo-scientific claptrap, leg art, human interest trivia, mindless prattle, tasteless enormities dredged up from the gutters of life. The "Gospel according to St. Randolph" reached thirty million readers, if you can call them readers. At least they read the comics. He had to retrench during the Depression, due to widespread boycotts and the Peoples Committee Against Hearst, and make do with only seven palaces and twenty papers. Advertising revenues and circulation were down, but his movie reviews were bought and paid for.

Although he usually lost at Monopoly, in real life Hearst owned more homes and castles than he had time to live in. His California fief at San Simeon was an architectural stew. Aldous Huxley called it "a monument to a faulty pituitary." There was no water atop the hill at San Simeon, but there was money. Result: seventy-eight bathrooms and some of the biggest swimming pools in the Western world. Ain't money wonderful? The place was infested with dachshunds—Hearst looked to them for companionship. And it had a zoo of exotic animals who ate better during the Depression than many people did. At San Simeon Hearst entertained celebrities and pontificated from his paper throne. His other California place was called Wyntoon, but to Miss Davies it was "Spittoon."

Old age found him still aspiring to maturity. Perhaps if he'd lived another decade? But even in his eighties, Hearst gave no sign of being a late bloomer. His ideas hardened with his arteries, but he remained a screwball to the end. Always a maniac with stage fright. You have to give him some credit, he was never dull. His towering mediocrity may never be equaled. He was a genius at the art of ballyhoo. Although he failed at most of what he tried to do, Hearst had great fun trying. He was "the champion loser of his time," said Swanberg, "unrivaled in the magnificence of his failure." His life proves that there is money in failure. Or at least a good time.

III

Bloodsuckers

Ivan the Terrible

Pirates

Boss Tweed

John D. Rockefeller

Ivan the Terrible

Ivan IV was the first terrible czar of Russia, but there were others. Some historians think he was only so-so, but his Russian name, *Groznyi*, translates as "Terrible" or, more precisely, "Awful." When he was bad he was awful.

As a child he was Ivan the Terrified, as he was scared out of his wits most of the time. Orphaned at age seven, he was assigned a guardian, but had him eaten by dogs. Why was this not seen as a red flag? Displaying an early aptitude for mindless cruelty, Ivan amused himself by torturing dogs and cats, hurling them from the high towers of the Kremlin so he could watch their bones break on the rocks below. He didn't mean any harm by it; he was only practicing, preparing for his future career as czar of Russia and vicar of Christ on earth.

Young Ivan enjoyed beating people with sticks, running amok, brawling, trampling old people with his horse. His favorite hobbies were hunting and debauching, but he did his homework and mastered traditional Russian tortures, as well as some new ones of his own invention. Soon he could boil people, fry them like omelets, hang them, decapitate them, drown them, strangle them, quarter them, impale them, blow them up and hack them to pieces. By 1547 he was ready for his coronation.

He liked to make the punishment exceed the crime. When blood splashed on Ivan, he would shout, *"Hoyda! Hoyda!"* This is Turkish, meaning "Giddyap" or "Let's go!" It was said that Ivan laughed at executions, even when they were not particularly funny.

At age seventeen Ivan married Anastasia Zakharin-Yuriev, his true love, and his behavior changed, becoming almost human at times. In those days women were believed not to have souls, but Anastasia was exceptional. Ivan suspected that she just might have one, maybe even as big as a man's. I can't say for sure. But she must have been special to survive thirteen years of marriage to him. Ivan made himself czar but, luckily, marital bliss left him little time for state duties.

Meanwhile, there were those awful Tatars to deal with. Mongol riffraff who liked to invade Russia from time to time and steal Russians into slavery. Not known for military valor, Ivan failed to distinguish himself at the siege of Kazan, but every winter he would go there and make faces at the godless Tatars, who would respond by lifting their robes and showing him their bare backsides (not really bare—they were covered with lice). Eventually he got tired of the bare backsides, as who wouldn't, and took Kazan in 1552. Four years later he took Astrakhan and there wasn't a bare bottom to be seen in the whole Volga valley. The Tatars mostly fled. A few stayed and became just folks, but kept their bottoms covered after that.

Then in 1560 his dear, sweet, loving wife died, and the light went out in Ivan's heart. Believing she had been poisoned, Ivan blew his lid and became "the Scourge of God." No more Mr. Nice Guy! Something snapped in his superego, loosing the base instincts of his id. His wailing and lamentations were pathetic to hear. This was the beginning of the period of Russian history known as "the Terror."

A pious man,[61] Ivan converted many godless heathens to Christianity by beating and whipping them until they had religious experiences. People always get religious if you beat them enough. He was devoted to the church and rarely missed Mass. He made lists of his male victims so monasteries could pray for their souls, at least until they became too numerous to keep track of.[62] Ivan composed prayers and church music and never ate meat during Lent. He was known to beat his forehead on the ground with pious ferocity, but had archbishops, metropolitans, and abbots eaten by bears or mauled by dogs, and he liked to loot churches. Ivan's faith "followed crooked lines," said Iswolsky. So did Ivan's mind.

In 1564 he fled Moscow, leaving no forwarding address. He wanted to get away from it all so he started a monastic community at Alexandrovskaya Sloboda and made himself abbot. But duties of state followed him. Between matins in the morning and vespers at night there were prisoners to be flogged, virgins to be deflowered, serfs to be mistreated, miscreants to be impaled, more dogs and cats to be hurled over the walls.

A czar's work was never done, so Ivan started the Oprichniki, his own personal band of degenerate cutthroats, to help out. The Oprichniki were supposed to make the boyars behave. The boyars were ignoble nobles who wanted to rule Russia in place of Ivan. By some

---

[61] But he called the pope a wolf.
[62] There was no need to keep track of female victims because they had no souls to fret about.

accounts, they were worse than he was! Ivan had some of them beheaded so they could think about it. He believed that Russia would never amount to anything ruled by effete boyars. It needed a lean, mean autocratic machine like him. Ivan believed in keeping boyars in their place: impaled on stakes.

Eventually he decided that the monastic life was not for him. His vocation left him when the stench of so many unburied corpses became unbearable. And besides, it was almost time to sack Novgorod. By 1569 Ivan had grown bored with torturing individual people and started punishing whole families, then whole towns. It was more efficient. Ivan sacked Novgorod in 1570 because its people were too friendly with the Poles, but he didn't have anything against the place. Didn't he honeymoon there in 1572?

Ivan did not like to sort out his victims. A nest of hornets cannot be separated, he said. So he exterminated them all, including their friends, relatives, neighbors, servants, children, dogs, cats, pet goldfish, etc. True to his name, he was terribly thorough.

Ivan often suspected that his subjects didn't like him, but you didn't hear any complaints, except from a few people who no longer had tongues. Boris Godounov suggested that Ivan try getting his way by being nice. Nothing came of it. Ivan did not know how to be nice.

Eventually the Oprichniki got to be a blot on Ivan's image, which was mostly blot anyway. He thought they were giving him a bad name, so he disbanded them. Sure, they were effective at subduing women and children, but helpless against Mongol invaders and not much use against boyars.

Ivan married again several times, but never again found true love. He wanted to marry Queen Elizabeth of England, mainly because he had never met her. He may have been attracted to her big navy.[63] English women were considered exotic in those days. She turned him down, thinking she could do better, so he called her a *poshlaya devitsa* (common slut). "I spit on you and your palace," he told her, undiplomatically. She was not the marrying kind anyway.[64] Later he proposed to her grandniece. He sent spies and ambassadors to England, but

---

[63] Also to her saltpeter, gunpowder, lead, brimstone, and military technology.
[64] Bess told him he would be welcome in England if he paid rent.

never saw them again. They all defected, just as he would have.

Ivan was not in great demand as a marriage match. He once tried to swap Estonia and Reval for Princess Catherine of Poland, but no deal.[65] Ivan ordered his father-in-law to find him an English wife, but it was not to be, so he had to make do with Russian wives and Livonian concubines. We don't know what he was like in bed, but one of his wives died after sixteen days of marriage to him. Some say he scared her to death. Ivan boasted of deflowering a thousand virgins, so we know he was either a liar or worse.[66] His table manners also left something to be desired, even if you ignored what he was eating.

War in Livonia was traditional in his family and Ivan invaded because it was there, and because he wanted access to the Baltic Sea and English women. He wanted a "window to the West" and a doorway to Western women. His fondest wish was to retire to safety in England with an English wife and the Russian treasury. But his Livonian adventure was disastrous. Ivan had to be continually at war because he did not want to pay his troops. They lived off the land and he preferred that they did it off someone else's land.

While he was in the West, those pesky Tatars sacked Moscow again. Ivan felt that something should be done about them. Unfortunately he could do nothing himself, as he was in hiding at Vologda, 330 miles away, with his treasure and twenty thousand of his best troops. He preferred to observe enemy movements from a safe distance—at least three hundred miles. A timid person, Ivan was forever trembling and running away, even when

---

[65] Would you marry a strange man whose surname was *Terrible*?

[66] Ivan must have lots of descendants alive today, but they don't seem to want to talk about him.

no one was chasing him.[67] Who would be foolish enough to chase him? But he always kept informed about Russia's wars so he would know when to come out of hiding and return to Moscow to take credit for the victory.

Ivan was a God-fearing man. In fact, he was afraid of practically everybody. King Stephen Batory of Poland thought the average hen more valiant than Ivan, who was afraid of witches, ghouls, sorcerers and ghosts.[68] They were afraid of him too. Ivan was afraid of his own grandmother, Anna Glinsky, a notorious witch. She used to change into a magpie and fly over Moscow, until Ivan made it illegal to do so. It got on his nerves when she did that! How would you like it if your grandmother did that?

In fairness to Ivan, we should mention his good qualities, if he had any. It is said that he did good things for Russia but no one knows what they were, as the archives were destroyed in a fire in 1626. Bobrick says that it must be said in Ivan's favor that "unlike Henry he executed none of his wives." Well, he had no need to execute wives, as nunneries were available for wives whose charms had all been a terrible mistake.[69] Besides, there are the allegations that he poisoned one wife and drowned another. Ivan was not a cannibal, at least not on fast days or during Lent, though he drove the Russian people to cannibalism.

It is true that he relieved the poor of their suffering, by killing them. That he was impartial in his administration of justice, punishing the innocent as well as the guilty. That he enriched the Russian Church by creating a bumper crop of new martyrs. That he unified Russia, much as Bismarck was to unify Germany.

Russia added vast new territories during Ivan's reign, but mainly because of the hordes of peasants who ran away from his "reforms." So it seems silly to credit

---

[67] Ivan *did* have enemies, even if they were imaginary.
[68] But wet hens have more courage than sense.
[69] Or had yielded to gravity.

him for the acquisition of Siberia. Ivan left Russia bankrupt, in a state of anarchy, its tax base depleted by wholesale flight of taxpayers, who preferred to deal with godless Tatars in the outback rather than with him. Can you blame them? We don't know how many people he killed because there were no high-speed computers in those days and women were not counted at all.

One day in 1581, Ivan killed his own son with a big, pointed staff, but didn't really mean to. He was sorry afterwards and said so. He liked his son OK; they used to have fun together, swapping mistresses and torturing people. The murder was sort of an accident,[70] but it made Ivan feel more godlike. After all, didn't God also sacrifice his own son, on the cross?

By 1576 Ivan had decided that torturing people was tiresome and he'd rather sleep. He was not himself anymore and besides, he had made his point. Then in 1584 he gave the Russian people the greatest gift he could give them—his own demise. Although his death brought instant relief it failed to bring peace, for it only started the period of dynastic conflict known as the "Time of the Troubles." As if there had been no troubles before that! On his deathbed Ivan repented some of his more revolting sins, reduced taxes, and became a monk, Brother Jonah, but few people remember him as Brother Jonah. Ivan believed he was God's *kluchnik* (vessel), but God was not available to confirm this.

Everyone in his line of succession was dead except his feeble-minded son Fyodor, who couldn't cut a figure in court, much less cut off heads. A sacristan by nature, Czar Fyodor loved to ring church bells. That was all he wanted from life. He had a perpetual idiotic grin on his childish face. Naturally, the Russian people loved him. He was so very, very harmless.

---

[70] His son got in the way while Ivan was kicking his pregnant daughter-in-law.

Ivan has been called a loathesome bloodsucker who devoured Christian flesh, but this may not be technically true. He didn't suck blood, he drank it. For all we know, Ivan may have been only trying to make a living. If you are wondering why the church did not exorcise Ivan, my guess is that exorcists were afraid of him.

Wipper called Ivan "one of the greatest diplomats of all time." Typical of Ivan's diplomacy was the letter he sent to Sigismund Augustus, King of Poland, informing him that a hole had been dug in the earth for his severed head.

What was troubling Ivan? It wasn't coffee nerves—he didn't drink coffee. Some say he was mad with mercury poisoning or painful arthritis. Others say he was just mad. Or he may have been just no damned good. Historians can only speculate on whether Prozac might have helped. Ivan said, "The cords of my soul and my body have been stretched too tight." Indeed, I know the feeling!

Blackbeard

Pirates

Piracy was known as "turning Turk" or "going on the account." It is the third oldest profession, after whoring and healing. During its "Golden Age" (1692-1725), practically everybody and his cousin were involved in it, directly or indirectly. Yes, even *your* ancestors—don't look so innocent! Not all pirates were hell-raising outcasts, lewd and blasphemous fellows. Some were gentlemen with urbane demeanors. You wouldn't know them on the street from apothecaries' clerks. Some had clean fingernails and wore clean underwear.

After all, successful pirates had more money than the great landlords of the peerage, more than the governor of the East India Company. Rome was founded by no better. Didn't Black Bart's crew call themselves "The House of Lords"? The Third Earl of Cumberland was a pirate with a master's degree from Cambridge. He carried in his hat a glove from Queen Bess. Captain Hook was educated at Eton and Balliol, according to J. M. Barrie. Indeed it was a blurry line that separated pirates from respectable businessmen, especially in hard times.

But some pirates were unsavory, it is true. Rumor has it that they swore and were not always monogamous. Some had bad teeth and didn't floss. Some were so awful they could have made a fortune in Hollywood. Sure, they would have been typecast—so was Lassie—but they would have been stars! With fan clubs and paparazzi even!

There was much to recommend a career in piracy. The money was good, though not steady. Anyway, it paid better than honest work. A man could be hanged for stealing a shilling, so why not steal more? It was more cost-effective. The hours were flexible, with no time clocks to punch. There were no union dues to pay, no taxes, no nagging wives. Malagasy women were good lovers; they would do it with practically anybody, even a pirate with a homemade prosthetic limb and no teeth. Winters could be enjoyed in tropical climes, with wine, women, and song. Madagascar was where the action was, for a while. During the Golden Age there was a hell of a party at New Providence in the Bahamas. It went on for five years, until Governor Rogers broke it up. But what a bash while it lasted! A tropical Gin Lane! New Providence was not a bad place, once you got used to the smell.

Women find pirates attractive because they like to reform cruel, heartless villains by giving them the love they never had. Especially good-looking villains like Errol Flynn or Douglas Fairbanks Jr. For pirates who were not good-looking, strumpets were available for debauching with in port towns.

But there were drawbacks as well. Pirates had no pension plans—nor any need for them. There was the possibility of abrupt retirement at the end of a noose (known as neck-stretching at Tyburn). Severance pay was meager: only five hundred pieces of eight for a severed limb. Pay was unsteady. "No prey, no pay" was the rule. The menu was not always dainty, unless you fancied cold maggots, dog meat, rats, boiled caterpillars, salmagundi, or moldy biscuits. There was the possibility of being marooned on a desert island without your favorite book. There was no "smoaking" on deck after 8:30 p.m. and no debauching of captive women without permission from the quartermaster. Occasional overtime was mandatory, and the pox was rampant. Flogging was another drawback, and guinea worms, malaria, gangrene, scurvy. But the biggest drawback was the company pirates had to keep.

So be sure to consider all the pros and cons before you decide on a career in pirating. You might want to take some aptitude tests to find out if you are mindless enough to succeed at it. It is not recommended for nervous Nellies or people with superegos. If security is your goal, you should reconsider bookkeeping or chicken farming, as nothing is guaranteed to pirates. Only the best few can expect to rise to the top and become emperors or presidents. Today the best career opportunities are in Hollywood.

A pirate needed good sea legs,[71] the gift of grab, and at least one earring. If you want to be an authentic pirate, you must learn to hate the Spanish—it is traditional.[72] Cussing and spitting are helpful. Pirates should try to act tough, especially female pirates. Parrots are optional, except in Hollywood. Growling "aarrrgg" will do more harm than good when *you* do it. Traditional pirates had

---

[71] But peg legs are acceptable in Hollywood.
[72] If you *are* Spanish you should hate the British, or at least the French.

venereal diseases, at least the pox, but it is not required. Ideally, a pirate should have access to a boat.

As I said, piracy was no profession for fussy eaters. The cook had the hardest job on a pirate ship. How many ways are there to serve rat meat?[73] No French name could render pirate food palatable. It took real creativity. The usual fare was salmagundi, also known as "clean-up-the-kitchen stew." It was highly seasoned—it *had* to be. Plus cackle-fruit (eggs) and high-protein hard tack (the protein came from the resident weevils). Washed down with beer, grog, or rumfustian. Pirates did not often add gunpowder to their rum, as it was useful for other things. In lean times, pirates had to eat whatever was available, but regardless of the menu, they ate like a kennel of hounds. Chinese pirates sprinkled themselves with garlic water for protection against bullets. It was not always effective, but did tend to keep adversaries farther away.

There were pirates to suit every taste. Privateers were legal; they had permission to prey upon politically-incorrect ships, such as those of bad guys or rich infidels. Some were even sponsored by churches. But their victims often failed to appreciate the difference between pirates and privateers. Indeed, there was very little difference when nobody was watching. Buccaneers were legal at first, meat dealers to passing ships, no more debased than your average neighborhood butcher. They butchered only cows until the Spanish ousted them from Hispaniola. Buccaneers were better than the French, said Pere Labat, a Jesuit, in 1694.

Picaroons were slavers, a bad bunch! But some pirates were themselves runaway slaves. Freebooters were Protestant and Dutch. Corsairs worked the Mediterranean. Arab corsairs considered it a cardinal sin to rob the living, but guess how they got around this taboo. That's right! Uskoks were commissioned by the devil. They regarded piracy as a religious duty. Gujarati

---

[73] Even the Royal Navy sometimes dined on rat stew.

89

rovers made captives drink an emetic of tamarindi and sea water to induce them to vomit up pearls and gems. It didn't do much good unless they already had pearls or gems inside. Barbary pirates specialized in making faces and whooping like wild Turks. Pirates of Penzance specialized in whooping like opera singers. Vikings were Scandinavian. So you see, just about everybody got in on the fun.

Black Bart had an illustrious career, capturing more than four hundred ships, most in the Caribbean, and still found time for foppery. He won most of the best-dressed pirate awards. He tried being an honest seaman, but felt it did not offer sufficient opportunity for advancement. "A merry life and a short one" was his motto. Black Bart was a big-time pirate, a real sea dog. Small-time pirates like Calico Jack Rackam were known as sea pups or "courtly seamen." Calico Jack preyed upon fishing boats. He must have liked fish.

Blackbeard was a bad one, alias Edward Teach or the Devil Incarnate. He looked like a fury from hell—or Hollywood. He liked to kill for the hell of it, and play risky games. He was a hard drinker; even fourteen wives couldn't civilize him. Hollywood would have loved him. Legend has it that his headless corpse swam around the Royal Navy sloop *HMS Pearl* several times before sinking from sight. It did no such thing! Blackbeard's murder brought howls of protest from respectable Carolina merchants, to whom he had brought prosperity.

Pirate flags conveyed important information. The Jolly Roger meant your luck had run out. The Jolly Roger plus a national flag meant privateers. A red flag meant no quarter given, or exact change only. A triangular flag with the word *Pittsburgh* meant last place in the National League. A lowered flag meant surrender. Lowered trousers meant trouble.

Pirates had to be prepared to move on short notice, as the typical pirate ship was no match for the Royal Navy. Cleanups happened, usually when pirates cut too much into the profits of the local merchants. Pirates were bad guys because they robbed for their own selfish gain; the Royal Navy were good guys because they robbed for others, mostly kings and queens. Christopher Columbus said that he who has gold has "the means of purchasing souls from purgatory," but this was not the usual motive of pirates. In some ports, pirates were welcome, as they tended to keep the French away.

There were degrees of piracy. Vasco da Gama, for example, is usually not considered a pirate, though he behaved like one at times. Indeed, don't we all? Piracy should be judged in the context of prevailing conditions on land. Could you live on forty honest shillings per year? Honesty won't pay the rent, and has no food value.

Bristol and Plymouth in England were favorite haunts of pirates like Drake, Ralegh, Hawkins, and the sea dogs, who shared Plymouth harbor with the queen's navy. Queen Elizabeth liked pirates, as they brought her a good return on her money. She even knighted Drake, who had singed King Philip's beard in Spain. She had only to unmuzzle him to keep the Spanish in check.

A few pirates became heroes, such as John Paul Jones, Jean LaFitte, and Honus Wagner. Other notable pirates were Prince Rupert, Captain Blood, Blind Pew, and Captain Kidd. This last was not as bad as you think. He had a commission from King William III so he should have been covered. Anyway, he didn't really mean it. Contrary to the 1952 movie, Captain Kidd never did actually meet Abbott and Costello.

Silver screen pirates like Tyrone Power and Burt Lancaster are not to be taken too seriously. They were not true pirates, as they did not kill real people or eat real dog meat. Besides, Hollywood takes liberties with the facts. Hollywood pirate ships are larger than real pirate ships to accommodate cameras, dueling, and swashbuckling on deck. And they smell better too, because their piss tubs are hardly ever used.[74] Pirate ships carry two crews. In Hollywood, second crews are known as understudies.

By 1850, pirates were having a hard time keeping up with steam-powered ships, but there are still pirates today. They steal boring things like credit cards, computers, Walkmans, Ovaltine, cigarettes, and oil tankers. Modern pirates do not kill for lentils. They use computers and cell phones and wear jogging suits, plastic flip-flops, army surplus, Levi's, sun glasses. It is hard to tell them from tourists. Corporate raiders wear neckties, but most pirates do not dress for success.

Mary Reade, a lady pirate

---

[74] Pirates in Barbara Cartland novels don't use piss tubs.

There were lady pirates as well, not to be outdone. If captured, they could "plead their bellies" to escape the noose. Anne Bonny was romanced by Calico Jack Rackam. A good thing too, as she was spared execution because of her pregnancy. Known as "Spitfire," she specialized in howling like a banshee and favored the death penalty for piracy, as she did not like competition.

Women pirates were of two types: those who did it and those who did not. Those who did not usually dressed in breeches and passed as boys in the crew. Some of them "smoaked" pipes. The powder rooms on pirate ships were not for ladies. They were called magazines, like the *Reader's Digest*. On some politically-incorrect pirate ships, women were not even allowed. Cheng I Sao (1775-1844) was a woman pirate who did it whenever she pleased, even with her adopted stepson. A toothless terror, she commanded thousands of other pirates and dominated the South China Sea.

Pirate ships needed to be careened periodically, as don't we all? The barnacles and worms had to be scraped off. A pirate's work was never done. Frequent careening gave pirate ships a speed advantage over merchant ships, until the latter cheated by using steam power.

Most pirates did not enjoy pirating. They did it for the money. They thought it was better than splitting codfish for a living. If you offered them honest work, some pirates would take it, along with anything else not nailed down. If you offered them fat pensions, pirates would accept them. Some might even stop pirating. We don't know how many would stop because pirates do not respond to poll questions. They are afraid of incriminating themselves. Can you blame them? Pompey the Great tried to reform pirates by offering them honest work; his own son turned Turk. Some pirates appear to be beyond redemption. You have to get them young, before age seven or eight. There are no twelve-step programs to reform pirates, as it would require more than twelve steps. When all the romance is boiled away, piracy is just plain old thievery. Just maritime mugging, a sordid business.

A few pirates retired with official pardons, but did not always live happily ever after, as pardons were not good for credit in grocery stores or liquor stores.

Piracy declined when the risks came to outnumber the profits. White-collar crime pays better now, so why bother? But pirates are like death and taxes and dogs. As long as there are needs and greeds, there will be people who think the world is up for grabs.

Boss Tweed

Like any normal American boy, little Billy Tweed wanted to be a fireman when he grew up, so he could wear red shirts and dash about New York City making lots of noise. But after dropping out of school at age eleven he learned from his father how to make chairs. He also taught himself how to use his fists and swear like a trooper. Showing an early predilection for plunder, he became adept at stealing potatoes and pigs' tails from shops a mile or more from home. It was more fun than making chairs, and he was darn good at it.

After beating up an urchin at age eleven for calling him "Little Bill," he was known as "Big Bill." Later "Big

Bad Bill" or "Boss." Eventually he came to be known as "the Great Malefactor" or "the Vulture" or, simply, "the Essence of Urban Rot."

The fire department was fun for a while, until he got kicked out in 1850—something about attacking a rival fire company on its way to a fire. Then he got into ward politics and discovered how corrupt it could be.[75] Seeing no reason to change it, he sat on a common council known as "the Forty Thieves." Feeling right at home among the thieves, he said, "A politician in coming forward takes things as they are." And why not?

Tweed thought he and his pals deserved a cut out of city expenditures, a percentage, out of consideration for their selfless services. Call it a commission or a gratuity or a kickback. Or call it tribute. Or call it pork. Call it whatever you like, "the Forty Thieves" padded bills and skimmed contracts, as needed. Did you expect these guys to work for nothing?

"Bell-ringing" was fun. This was announcing bills that would cost somebody money. When that somebody heard the "bell" ringing, he or she would offer to bribe "the Forty Thieves" to get the bill killed. And their bribes were always graciously accepted—if they were big enough.

The thieves once submitted a bill to the comptroller that might have been a bit padded. It claimed that each councilman had consumed, at one sitting, eight pounds of beef, a chicken and a half, 225 oysters, a pound of sausage, two pounds of ham and three loaves of bread, followed by the smoking of one hundred cigars. I can't say for sure it was padded; I wasn't there. I suppose Tweed could have done it, he was world-class. His body gave evidence of considerable padding.

Already by 1853 there were problems with uppity newspapers and a reform party. Tweed denied everything

---

[75] Tweed was a Soft-Shell Democrat. There were also Hard-Shells, Whigs, Woolyheads, Hunkers, Drys, Barnburners, Know-Nothings, Locofocos. Plus others too silly to mention.

but his beady eyes told a different story, so he escaped to Washington and sat heavily in Congress for a term. But it was not the same. He missed the New York lobbyists. As a little fish in a big pond, he was not offered enough temptations to make it interesting. He did not like being a little fish, and he did like temptations.

So he returned to New York, where he was not the only corruptionist in town. It was Fernando Wood who set the pace, but Tweed hated Wood, fearing he would leave nothing for him to steal. So he tried to get rid of Wood—and got a reputation as a reformer!

Tweed did not consider it corruption, what he did, preferring to call it "enterprise" or "playing the game." Indeed, his system of accounting was enterprising. Bribes paid out were entered under "legal expenses." Bribes paid in were for "legal services." Bribes to newspapers were charged to "advertising." Bribery was known as "taking care of people," but was not as Christian as all that. The house he built for his little blond friend was entered under "coach house." Well, maybe she was his coach!

Having blown all his money on the 1860 election, Tweed declared bankruptcy, but recovered soon enough. He had no trouble getting himself re-elected, as he soon had ample money to buy votes. At election time he would manufacture voters by wholesale naturalizations of immigrants fresh off the boat from God knows where. His supporters voted early and often. When asked how many fraudulent votes were cast, Tweed couldn't say for sure. "It would need a man higher up in arithmetic than I am to do that," he admitted. But his corruption was not confined to election day. Lynch says it "began on the first day of January and ended on the last day of December."

He could count on the Irish vote because he scorned the Know-Nothing Party. He helped Jews because the Jewish vote was bigger than the bigot vote. He had the support of the Bowery Boys in the Seventh Ward and the Dead Rabbits in the Sixth. He kept the poor supplied with firewood in the wintertime and they kept him supplied with votes on election day.

Tweed had some admirable qualities:

* He liked his mother.

* He waltzed divinely, and liked canaries and flowers.[76]

* His eyes sparkled. So what if they were beady?

* He was generous with what did not belong to him.

* He was loyal to fellow scoundrels.

* He bought shoe laces from disabled veterans.

* He bought Christmas dinners for poor people who could vote.

* He supported his ten children, plus uncounted mistresses.

* He supported charities, some of which actually existed.

But people did the math: how did he put by ten million dollars in seven years on a salary of $7,500 per year? It did not add up. How did he give his daughter such a lavish wedding so soon after declaring bankruptcy?

As commissioner of public works, Tweed worked over the public. The courthouse in Manhattan was known as the Tweed Building or "the house that Tweed built" because so much of its cost overrun went into his pocket. Its cuspidors must have been state-of-the-art; they cost $190 apiece! The benches were not the only thing about it that was padded. Tweed bought a quarry in Massachusetts. Guess where the overpriced marble in the courthouse came from.

There were more problems with the press, although most papers were silenced easily enough by city advertising revenues or "subsidies." Horace Greeley and the *Tribune* were nuisances, as was cartoonist Thomas

---

[76] But in court Tweed looked like a cat that had just swallowed a canary.

Nast, but it was George Francis Train who claimed the distinction of being the first person to suggest that Tweed be hanged.

The Tweed ring was so called because it encircled enough corrupt politicians of both parties to control both party machines, like a ring around a bi-partisan bathtub. Tweed had no partisan agenda. He was willing to co-operate with anybody who co-operated with his plundering.

The ring began as a plot to get Tweed and his cronies elected to all the important offices, from which they would put through a new charter, because who could stop them? It worked. Acting as a filter, the ring diverted a third of city expenditures into its own pockets, later half, then two thirds. If that still wasn't enough, there were fictitious firms and contractors clamoring to be paid, as were the dead people kept on the payroll for old times' sake. How did they get away with it? They audited themselves! The new charter made Tweed auditor, a job he did with all the dedication of a fox guarding a hen house.

Tweed had fans who wanted to erect a statue of him, but he squelched the idea, fearing it would expose him to ridicule, and to pigeons. At 280 pounds, he was a large target. Some have argued that Tweed was not so bad, only a victim of irresponsible journalism, but Tweed himself called his life "terrible and wicked" and he should have known. He was there, I believe him! He went beyond honest graft. When asked by a reporter if he had stolen the people's money, Tweed replied, "This is not a question one gentleman ought to put to another." Notice that he did not answer the question. Or did he? Tweed was no Robin Hood. Yes, he did rob the rich and give to the poor, but he also robbed the poor and gave to the rich.

Meanwhile, cartoonist Nast was depicting Tweed as a bloated vulture feasting on the people's money. "Let's stop them damned pictures," grumbled Tweed, whose supporters could barely read but were adept at looking at pictures. Tweed thought Nast's cartoons were . . . well, nasty! He wanted to horsewhip Nast. He decided that Nast needed a rest in Europe for a few years, but Nast was not tired, and continued turning out "them damned pictures."

Tweed spread his patronage far and wide. He had twelve "manure inspectors" on his payroll, and an "interpreter" who could neither read nor write. Plus dog walkers paid by the city. But he missed a few disgruntled soreheads, who turned against him and started leaking evidence to George Jones, the new editor of the *Times*. Jones thought he could fight City Hall, maybe even

Tammany Hall[77] and Mayor Hall. The fun began when the *Times* began reporting the facts in lurid detail. Never before were so many people fascinated by bookkeeping figures. It was better than the sports page! Tweed began to get nervous, and transferred property to his son Richard.

When the bubble burst, Tweed's disciples scattered in all directions. An injunction put a stop to his spending, but he did not go hungry even then, as people pelted him with cabbages and potatoes. He had come a long way from his youth, when he'd had to steal such items.

Tweed was arrested and sent to Blackwell's Island, where he was treated as a big fish. Too bulky to fit into a normal prison cell, he was given luxurious quarters near the ladies' sewing room in the keeper's apartment building. Here he had flowered cretonne curtains, a servant, and full privileges.[78]

One day, when the prisoner was visiting his wife in the city, he gave his keepers the slip. How could such a fat man vanish into thin air? the public wanted to know. Tweed sightings were the rage for a while, until he was recaptured in Spain, disguised as a common sailor. His disguise fooled no one; he still looked like a bloated vulture. The Spanish authorities identified him from a Nast cartoon! "Them damned pictures" again!

Back in jail in New York, Tweed pined for the fat living of the good old days. He decided to come clean and confess everything, in exchange for his freedom, but his testimony incriminated practically everybody, so he was not freed. We don't know how much money he stole—you couldn't count that high anyway. He said he needed the money to buy votes in Albany. Was it his fault that they cost so much? He wanted to pay it all back, but how could

---

[77] A social club that became anti-social.
[78] Tweed had been an Odd Fellow, but became a regular fellow in prison because he could no longer afford to pay his dues.

he? His only marketable skill was graft! He was not allowed to do his old job of borrow, spend, and keep some for yourself. He was not allowed to sell legislation. So most of the money was never recovered. Taxpayers picked up the bill.

Tweed passed beyond the custody of the New York sheriff on 12 April 1878 and was buried in Brooklyn. There was no sermon at his funeral. What was there to say? He was a difficult corpse to eulogize. But you should have heard the sermons in other pulpits around town, not to mention in the saloons. They went on for weeks! Now he has finally blown over.

Tweed did not invent corruption, or even sin. He only took them to their logical conclusions. It was fun while it lasted, but Nast made the Monarch of Manhattan into the Monarch of Tweedville, a cartoon character of lesser stature than Bugs Bunny or Krazy Kat. Tweed's life teaches us that you can't be too careful what you do and say in political cartoons.

John D. Rockefeller

John D. Rockefeller was born to keep books. If books had not existed, they would have had to be invented for him. Life was just a great big ledger to him. The purpose of life was to balance books, and then some.

He began his career in Cleveland at four dollars per week. You may well ask, "How did a four-dollar-a-week bookkeeper become the world's richest man?" "Efficiency," he explained. But can anyone be that efficient? When pressed he would admit, "The Good Lord gave me the money."

Taking after his father, "Devil Bill" Rockefeller, John D. kept "Ledger A" separate from the Bible. Having air-tight compartments in his soul for business and morality, he saw no reason why a robber baron could not also be a good Christian gentleman. After all, God put petroleum in the ground for a reason.[79] It would be a sin not to use it to illuminate the world. Besides, God needed the money! "If the apostle Paul were alive today, he would be a captain of industry," said John D., who considered himself an honest man. After all, he never cheated at golf. And didn't he always tell the truth when money was not involved? Did you ever see him mix benzine with his oil?

Deeply entrenched in the Protestant ethic, Rocky believed he was God's fiduciary. It was his solemn duty to grab as much money as he could, by whatever means, and give it to God. A deacon at the Euclid Avenue Baptist Church, he thought he was John the Baptist. As a matter of fact, he was!

He decided that petroleum was here to stay. You couldn't get rid of the mucky stuff anyway; it kept oozing out of the ground when you tried to mine salt. So why not put it to some use? His father had sold it as "medicinal rock oil," but John D. did him one better. He created the Standard Oil Company, one of the most powerful runaway monopolies of all time. Bigger than Boardwalk and Park Place with hotels!

The oil business was boom and bust at first. Producers would not co-operate in regulating production, so Rocky had to take over the whole industry. After that it was stable and steady, steady boom for Standard Oil, steady bust for everyone else. Standard Oil grew, and grew some more, eventually assuming the size and attributes of a sovereign nation. "A fine piece of brigandage," said muckraker Ida Tarbell.[80] Could it be that John D.'s methods were not entirely ethical?

Well, what of it? Business was war so what was the harm in a little cheating? Sure, Rocky weighed the price of wrongdoing, but decided to pay it. Why not? He was on

---

[79] But why did God put "skunk oil" under Ohio? It smelled like a pile of dead polecats.
[80] Known to John D. as "Miss Tarbarrel."

a mission for God. And the surplus value poured in. "When it's raining porridge," said his sister Lucy, "you'll always find John's bowl right side up." Some say he made bribes, but he denied this. "Grants" yes, but not bribes. Others say he made threats. Not threats, "timely advice," said Rocky, who was very creative about interpreting the spirit of the law.

The South Improvement Company was his first major break with decency. Who could argue with "improvement"? Its collusion with railroads was soon declared illegal, but not until it had forced competitors out of business or into the Standard Oil octopus. Everybody did it, said John D. Anyway, he was only doing unto others what they were trying to do unto him. Everybody did *not* do it, said Miss Tarbell. The weak did not prey upon the strong. Rocky did not invent railroad rebates[81] or even corruption, but he did ratchet them up higher than anyone else did. Monopoly was his goal, and he achieved it in 1879.

About that time Rocky became a fugitive from justice, forever dodging court subpoenas. They got to be nuisances! He had enemies who objected to his swallowing up the whole bloody industry. There were soreheads who refused on principle to do business with Standard Oil. For them there was Republic Oil, which cultivated retailers who loathed Rocky and his monstrous trust. How were they to know that Republic Oil was secretly owned by Standard Oil? Wasn't everything?

In 1888, a New York Senate committee likened Standard Oil to a disease spreading across America. In 1890, the Sherman Antitrust Act outlawed combinations in restraint of trade, but it came to be known as "The Swiss Cheese Act" because it was so full of holes. A mere nuisance.

When Jay Gould died in 1892 the title of the "World's Most Hated Man" came up for grabs. There were

---

[81] Railroad rebates later became "commissions."

many deserving candidates, of course, but the public wanted John D. to have it. After all, hadn't he earned it? Wasn't the title made for the likes of him? He was "the greatest criminal of the age," said Governor LaFollette. Miss Tarbell said he looked like a dead jellyfish, and wasn't it great fun to hate someone who looked like that? Rocky scorned public opinion. "Let the world wag," he would say, and by and large, it did. He refused to respond to criticism, fearing it would invite discussion. Meanwhile he sulked in private, all the way to the bank.

He claimed he had no need to deodorize his reputation by doing philanthropy, but he did it anyway, out of the kindness of his tender heart. He wanted to attack the root causes of human misery, at least those not arising out of his business practices, and he wanted to dodge taxes, of course. Taxes were like termites, eating holes in his profits. But philanthropy was a tricky business, as he did not want to subvert evolution by helping the weak or the needy. He didn't want to weaken the moral backbones of an army of beggars. He found philanthropy to be a complicated business, so he tended toward Baptist causes and the Anti-Saloon League.

Rocky did not really need his money. He ate like a church mouse and rode the El to work for a nickel. He never had any craving for tobacco, booze, wild women, or fat living, only money. Surplus value was never more surplus than his. He was not like working people, who squandered their wages on picture shows and silly fripperies.

His money was said to be "tainted,"[82] but it was good enough for most people. He gave lamps to the Chinese (to hook them on oil) and shiny new dimes to little children.[83] And in 1893 he bailed out the federal government. There were requests from all over to be

---

[82] 'Tain't yours and 'tain't mine.
[83] During the Depression he gave them nickels instead.

corrupted by Standard Oil funds, which were as popular as he was not.

In the 1890s John D. gradually faded into retirement, but his profits did not retire. Even on the golf courses, surplus value bombarded him more relentlessly than ever.

Theodore Roosevelt was a big game hunter and Standard Oil was big game, so he went after it, but it got away. Finally, in 1911, the Supreme Court busted it up into independent companies, but what good did that do? Our man Rocky owned shares in those independent companies and the parts proved to be more profitable than the whole! His profits became an avalanche that threatened to bury him alive. Was there no escape from all that money? His income was exploding, out of control.

Whatever could he do? Where could he hide? It was philanthropy or bust.

And so he became JDR, the source from whom oil blessings flowed, a crabbed, poker-faced, miserly old philanthropist! A reptilian incomepoop, leprous and diseased, wizened and bloodless. His pulse was only 52, you know. Was he a mummy? Was he even alive? Who cared? His money was alive and well.

Nobody called him Jack or Johnny. More likely they called him "the Grand Acquisitor" or "the Money Machine" or "the Sponge" or "the Octopus" or simply, "the Old Reprobate." But his philanthropy was noticed, and in time he became Saint Rocky, benefactor of all humankind.[84]

He was a great lover. In addition to his lifelong love affair with bookkeeping, he loved poetry, the Baptist Church, Sunday school picnics, golf, oil, and most of all, a good bargain. He also loved to sit with his back to the wall. He hated a few things as well, including red ink, income taxes, subpoenas, uppity competitors, unions, socialists, muckrakers and other soreheads. And Miss Ida "Tarbarrel," of course.

Rockefeller suffered from some peculiar formation of his brain, said Clarence Darrow. Some said he was a clinical case of obsessive-compulsive disorder. Others that he had a problem with toilet training, but we won't go into that here. He was not without talent, as he could balance crackers on his nose, then flip them into his mouth.

John D. left us these valuable tips:
* Hide the profits.
* Keep ears open and mouth shut.
* Watch out for missing barrel bungs. Take care of the bungs and the barrels will take care of themselves.
* Stay away from Demon Rum.

---

[84] Except spineless layabouts and the needy.

* Never buy politicians unless the price is right. Make sure they stay bought. Make them come to the back door. Pay them by certificate of deposit, never by check.
* Give competitors a "good sweating." Know everything about them and their in-laws, but don't hire spies unless they earn their keep.
* Always remember that a nickel is a whole year's interest on a dollar.
* Sleep with a revolver by your bed.
* Don't accept honorary positions that don't pay money.
* Fine your children one cent for being late for prayers. It adds up.
* Catch a good sermon once or twice a week. It will wind you up like a clock.
* Never use blackmail unless money is involved.
* Never read anything but newspapers, business reports, and the Bible.
* When practical, use legal means.
* Achieve monopoly. Do not pass GO without collecting two hundred dollars.

Rockefeller's environmental record left something to be desired, but in fairness it was not entirely his fault that Lake Erie became flammable. And the foul, acrid atmosphere over Cleveland was probably just one of those things.

Always the country boy in the big city, John D. refused to play the game of conspicuous consumption. He disdained yachts, titled snobs, *Louis Quatorze* furniture, old-money clubs, but owned five palatial homes.[85] His estate at Pocantico Hills, New York, was said to be an example of what God could do if she only had the money. And Rocky made it pay. "We make a small fortune out of ourselves," he said, "by selling to our New Jersey place, at $1.50 or $2.00 each, trees which originally cost us only

---

[85] He had to rotate homes seasonally to avoid taxes.

five or ten cents at Pocantico. We are our own best customers." I wonder, did he ever cheat himself? Undersell himself? Give himself rebates? Swallow himself up?

John D. was not all bad. As a philanthropist he was a notch or two higher than his father, a philanderer. At least he was not a horse thief, like his father. But was his good side as good as his bad side was bad? Not according to William Jennings Bryan, who thought Rocky belonged behind bars. Or to Miss Tarbell, who said charity was no substitute for fair play. He was a monster, said Helen Keller. But Mark Twain said that anyone who was hated that much could not be all bad.

John D. wanted to live to be a hundred, and damn near made it, but could not buy off death forever. He is now the patron saint of the Standard Oil Company. St. Rocky's feast day is May 23rd. But Rocky's money and descendants are still very much with us. They have insinuated themselves into practically everything. His tainted money is more popular than Jesus, but in the end he found, to his dismay, that money can't buy you love, if you look like a dead jellyfish.

IV

Jacks and Queens

Sir Walter Ralegh

Marie Antoinette

Otto von Bismarck

Queen Victoria

Sir Walter Ralegh

Walter Ralegh had a head full of moneymaking schemes, but could not make them pay. The only thing that paid was making eyes at a bald-headed queen old enough to be his mother, Queen Elizabeth I, known as Queen Bess or "the Iron Lady." So he made a career of it. The eyes had it.

Born in a house of mud and straw, he grew up with pigs and cattle. The Raleghs lived "like toads under a harrow," so is it any wonder that Walter wanted to get rich quick? He tried soldiering for Huguenots in France, but it did not make him rich, so he considered piracy. Why not? Didn't pirates make a good living? Didn't plunder pay?

In Dartmouth harbor he brushed up his pirating skills by seizing a Spanish fruit boat. By 1578 he thought he was ready for his first expedition of discovery to the New World, to be financed by piracy. It didn't work out, but got the attention of the queen.

The following year he was imprisoned for brawling, which again got the attention of the queen, who had been looking for people who liked to fight. She gave him a command in Ireland, where he could fight to his heart's content, with her royal blessing. Ireland was a hotbed of popery and a burden to the English Crown, which would have preferred to sink the whole island to the bottom of the sea and be done with it; but alas, the technology was not available to do so. Meanwhile, Walter's job was to exterminate the Irish, replace them with English transplants, and keep out those pesky Spanish and Portuguese Papists.

He butchered the Irish so efficiently that he came to be regarded as an expert on Irish affairs, but he did not like Ireland. It was "a lost lande," he moaned, not a commonwealth but a commonwoe. At four measly shillings per day, he would have preferred to be in England flirting with the queen.[86] That was where the money and the perks were. But Ireland was good practice for the New World. It was in Ireland that he perfected the art of hacking people to pieces.

In 1582 Ralegh proposed a plan to the queen to reduce her expenditures in Ireland. This was when he first came fully into the queen's eye, and she took mark of the man and his parts. Which parts in particular history does not say, but from that time he enjoyed fluttering and darting about the queen, and "burgeoning" in her presence. Ralegh must have been good-looking because the queen enjoyed having him around, and even became addicted to his brazen flattery. She didn't mind that he was morally challenged because she was too. Besides, morality was not very useful in those days. He was "damnably proud" and arrogant to everyone else, but willing to grovel shamelessly for the merest hint of a smile from his beloved fairie queen. She had sappy pet

---

[86] He kept some dead men on his payroll to help make ends meet.

names for all her male pets: Hatton was her "Mutton," Leicester was her "Sweet Robin." Ralegh was her "Water Rawly" or "Warter." Others were too disgusting to mention.

Ralegh wanted to colonize the New World, but how could he? He was not allowed out of the queen's presence. She could not manage for long without his flattery. He sent settlers to "Virginia" in 1585 but they ran out of granola and trail mix. Having exhausted the hospitality of the natives and having nothing to eat but uppowoc, they gave up and returned to England, ravenous for a good feed. Uppowoc was *nicotiniana rustica*, or *tobacco vulgaris* to us. It was not good eating so Ralegh tried smoking it and created a sensation at court. Soon peers were smoking themselves silly, but it is not true that Ralegh corrupted the morals of the queen by teaching her to smoke, as she had no morals to begin with.

He tried to colonize Virginia again in 1587, but failed again. His settlers disappeared and have not been heard from, as we go to press. Venture capital soon lost interest in them. What was Virginia good for, anyway? Sure it had tobacco and timber and turpentine and sassafras, but where was the gold? It was on Spanish galleons.

Ralegh was not much good as a pirate, never "of good happe" at sea. Inclined to seasickness, he preferred to take the footbridge over the river Thames rather than risk a wherry boat ride. But there was gold in the New World, he was sure of it. It was there for Spanish Papists, why not for English Protestants? So what if there was no bridge to get him there!

In 1591, another of his privateering schemes yielded him such a miserable profit that he complained, "Wee might have gotten more to have sent them a-fishinge." At this point he should have taken up fishing.

Meanwhile, the New World beckoned, and it was not nearly big enough to share with the Spanish, who claimed that the pope had given it to them. "Guiana is a country that hath yet her maidenhead," pondered Ralegh, with lewd intent. It was lying there, wantonly waiting to be violated by someone. Why not me? "The graves have not been opened for gold," he thought, not ruling out grave robbing. Never mind that the New World teemed with monsters, pestilences, and naked savages. A way must be found to make it pay. And if it did not pay, well, it was still a good place from which to plunder Spanish treasure ships.

Ralegh was more than a pirate. While other Englishmen were content to plunder Spanish ships, he wanted to plunder Spanish continents, before those wretched Papists did. He wanted to plant English Protestants in savage lands and watch them sprout. He wanted a Greater England across the seas because there was English gold in the New World, not to mention English tobacco, and English tribute money to be collected. Besides, the New World was a good dumping ground for Puritans, Brownists, undesirables, and other social detritus.

In 1588, Ralegh was supplanted from his role as top flirt by the Earl of Essex, the queen's new pet. But he was still allowed to flit and flutter about her until 1592, when he was caught committing a royal no-no, "being too inward" with one of the queen's maids. So inward, in fact, that the maid was with child. He was guilty as charged. She was Bess Throckmorton and I am inclined to forgive him this time because this Bess had "violet breath and lips of jelly, and the softest down on her belly." Plus, hair on her head! Can you blame him for being smitten? Their wooing was so passionate that it had to be described in French! And on the inside she was of "wantonness and wit." A suitable match for Wanton Walter!

So our naughty courtier was locked up in the Tower of London, where he went half mad when refused permission to see the hatchet-faced queen. This amorous swain still had his eye on his bottom line! Do we have an eternal triangle here? He had not one but *two* Besses to juggle. The queen was a saint of perfection, he insisted, not seeing too clearly through the bars. Her eyes surpassed the stars in clearness. Her hands were more white than ivory. Her wit turned nations upside down. He was smitten!

She was a bitch, said the Earl of Northumberland. Her carcass was crooked, said the Earl of Essex. "A fierce old hen," said Lytton Strachey. She had a "celestial frame,"[87] said Ralegh, with stars in his eyes. Ain't love wonderful?

Smoking himself silly

---

[87] So does *Ursa Major*.

While "in the walls captived," Ralegh at last had some luck. One of his ships captured a major prize in the Azores, the Portuguese carrack *Madre de Dios*, to the delight of the queen, who grabbed the lion's share of the booty. So Ralegh was ransomed, on a short leash, in order to supervise the looting of the ship, but still not allowed near the queen. Back home in Dorset in time for Christmas 1592, he behaved himself for a while, until ambition's tug became irresistible once again.

In 1595 he finally crossed the ocean, seasickness and all, to Guiana in South America, looking for the fabulous kingdom of El Dorado, and gold with which to woo back the queen's favor. Without success, as usual, but the book sold well, as there was much interest in crocodiles, naked savages, headless men, and bloodthirsty Amazons. The book was an infomercial intended to attract investors for another expedition, but it failed to impress them or the queen. Instead, Spanish Papists took such a lively interest in it that in 1596 the queen sent Ralegh to sack Cadiz and "enfeeble the king of Spain." In the process, Ralegh was wounded and too enfeebled himself to grab much loot. All he got out of it was a lame leg. Nevertheless, Queen Bess forgave him his sins and allowed him once again to burgeon in her royal presence.

Meanwhile, Ralegh's neighbors were complaining that his London home was a hotbed of plotting, scheming, witchcraft, atheism, freethinking, and God knows what else. His pals kept the neighborhood abuzz with gossip, and were accused of drying tobacco on the leaves of a Bible and even of denying the Trinity![88] The neighbors were right. Ralegh's home was the nerve center of his business and scientific schemes, good and bad. Stargazers, pirates, poets, wizards, mapmakers, mathematicians, and other suspicious characters were seen there. Lucifer himself was seen to come and go, according to some accounts.

---

[88] They claimed that he spelled the name of God backwards.

When Queen Bess died in 1603, still with no hair apparent, the good times were over for Ralegh, as the king who replaced her was not smitten with his male magnetism. Ralegh had nothing in common with King James, who liked Spaniards and regarded tobacco smoking as a "vile and stinking custom." Ralegh was not his type at all, and it wasn't long before he was back in the tower, accused of conspiring against the king. You'll have to decide for yourself whether he was guilty this time. If you ask me, he was treated rawly.

In the tower, Ralegh befriended young Prince Henry, the heir to the throne, hoping he would free him in due time. But the prince succumbed to typhoid fever, after drinking a cordial made by Ralegh. So our man was in for a long stretch this time, although his cordial was probably harmless enough. It was mostly sugar and herbs, and some magic powder, but I can't vouch for the bezoar stone in it. Never drink bezoar stone if you can help it. Always read labels!

Nevertheless, in March 1616 Ralegh was released from captivity for another expedition to Guiana, to find El Dorado or bust. King James was hoping that one of three things would happen:

* Ralegh would bring back lots of gold.
* Ralegh would be eaten by a crocodile.
* Ralegh would turn pirate or otherwise provide legal pretext to be properly hanged.

The first two didn't work out, so back into the tower he went. A born loser, he finally lost his head in 1618, for dubious reasons.[89] Stebbing says that King James later came to regret beheading Ralegh, but by then it was too late. Never behead anyone unless you are sure.

Although he failed at most of what he tried to do, Ralegh left his mark on the world.[90] His *Historie of the*

---

[89] Ralegh requested to be beheaded rather than hanged, and his wish was graciously honored.
[90] Despite spending a quarter of his manhood in jail.

World was one of the better histories written in the Tower of London in the first two decades of the seventeenth century. His poetry has been described as "dismal groans," but was not as bad as all that. It was passably OK—for a pirate—if you like political pandering and shameless flattery.[91] He made Guiana British and America English-speaking. But for Ralegh we might be speaking some barbarous, heathen language to this day! Americans owe Ralegh a special debt of gratitude for naming Virginia after his Virgin Queen. Otherwise we might be calling it Ossomocomuck or Wingandacon. He also gave us nicotine addiction, lung cancer, and his son, Wat Ralegh, who was crude, even by seventeenth century standards. Wat was born to be hanged, admitted his father, whose paternity was painfully obvious. About 1588, Ralegh introduced the potato to Ireland, and that one stuck. Without it the staple diet of the Irish, fish and chips, would be impossible today. Ralegh handed Queen Bess the first potato she had ever seen; she didn't know what to do with it.

But most of Ralegh's schemes failed miserably. El Dorado turned out to be a mythical kingdom, rich in mythical gold, but Ralegh had no use for mythical gold. Nor did the queen appreciate being named the empress of a mythical place. He never did find the fabled headless men or the bloodthirsty Amazons; they did not find him either. The English Crown didn't care about fool's gold, and wasn't convinced that cannibals, naked heathens, or headless men could ever become proper Englishmen. Ralegh did find oyster-bearing trees along the Orinoco River, or so he claimed, but where were the gold-bearing trees? Ralegh invested heavily in a voyage to find the fabled Northwest Passage, another mythical place. So it was disappointing, unless you like myths and fables.

---

[91] Some of Ralegh's poetry might not be his. We can't be sure who was to blame for most of it.

Although Ralegh was not stupid, he was not quite sure how to spell his own name.[92] He once signed a deed as "Rawleyghe," but usually got closer than that. The Spanish called him "Guatteral," because that's what he looked like to them, but Ralegh has been called worse. Henry Howard said that Ralegh was "worse than anything ever vomited up from hell." Not much good has ever been vomited up from hell.

People usually disliked Ralegh, considering him an overweening braggart—even worse than an underweening braggart. He had all the tact of a bull in a china shop. After the death of Essex in 1601, Ralegh became the most hated man in England, a title he held, off and on, for the rest of his life. But people still had to be nice to him, for fear that he might write a sonnet or an epigram about them. Shakespeare took some swipes at Ralegh in his plays, but disguised him under false names, even Spanish names!

Stebbing thought Ralegh a great man, but the Irish thought him a brute. I don't know how many corpses he left rotting in Ireland, so I can't say whether their total rose to the level of greatness.

Ralegh was amazingly versatile in his efforts to make a living. He ran the gamut, from poetry to piracy. From grave robbing to genocide to overseas real estate, he was in there trying. I still say he should have taken up fishing. And he had a natural aptitude for the butcher's trade. His life teaches us that abject groveling before middle-aged queens might pay for a while, but it's not steady. You might run out of queens. If you want to die with your head still attached, you'd be better advised to open a laundromat.

---

[92] Lacey assures us that Ralegh was the correct spelling. You'd better accept that and let's not fight about it.

Marie Antoinette

Marie Antoinette was not as bad as you think, and she didn't say, "Let them eat cake."[93] She didn't cause the French Revolution, not by herself anyway. It was not even her idea to get involved with the French in the first place. It was her Austrian mother, Maria Theresa, who led her to believe that Louis Auguste was a handsome prince who spouted flame through his nostrils. He was nothing of the sort!

The wedding cost nine million francs but the bills were never paid, so it was OK. It was a grand wedding, except for the bridegroom and the casualties. Dozens of

---

[93] I am not sure about this; I wasn't there when she didn't say it.

people were trampled to death during the festivities, which tended to put a damper on the fun.

The bridegroom, who became King Louis XVI, was known as "the Walking Stomach" or "the Fat Pig" or "the Great Booby" or "Louie the Last." Most of all he liked to eat, and in time became engulfed in fat.[94] He took his food very seriously, even to assigning armed guards to protect his meat. Otherwise he was devoid of any passion, except for shooting deer. He also liked to shoot cats—for sport, not for food. And he had an unfortunate tendency to do honest work with his hands, which was unbecoming in a king.[95] Her brother called him "a wet slab of fish." She called him "the poor man." He had nothing to offer but good intentions, and a throne to sit on. According to Castelot, her "body seemed made for love." And she was married to a wet slab of fish! Clearly, she had a problem!

But Louie was always in bed by eleven o'clock, so Marie Antoinette and her coterie of feather-brained layabouts made their plans accordingly. Sometimes they even cheated by moving the clock ahead. The fun began at eleven, without the snoring king, except for her "greeting the dawn" parties. But never mind the clock, they partied continuously, for years. And why not? They were aristos! It was their job!

In the daytime there were horse racing, faro and other card games, tric-trac, billiards, lotto, trashy novels, artless prattle, flirtations, etc. After dark there were maniacal suppers, operas, balls, more flirtations. Changing clothes consumed much of her time. She was bored with court ritual, playing the harpsicord, dull evenings with the pompous, gouty, old dowager aunts. She preferred dissipating with powder-headed youths. Wouldn't you?

---

[94] Those interested in a day-by-day account of his diet should read his journal.

[95] But brain work exhausted him.

123

The scandals began in 1775, when she discovered Paree! The chief suspect was Count Axel Fersen, a handsome Swede. Haslip says, "There can be little doubt that they became lovers." Others deny this. I can't say for sure; I wasn't there. But he gave her a sheepdog, so you know it was serious. There were other suspects; even the Duke of Dorset was not above suspicion! As we go to press, the paternity of her four children has still not been settled. "He belongs to the state," she said about her first son. She enjoyed pretty, featherbrained women as well. She was not stupid, but let her intelligence lie fallow for long periods of time. She was saving it for a rainy day.

In those days French female royals were mostly stiff-necked, dyspeptic, cankered old fossils, so it is no wonder that Marie Antoinette was likened to Venus or Hebe or "Psyche in the bloom of youth." Edmund Burke likened her to the morning star. The Helens and the Graces were streetwalkers in comparison, said Horace Walpole. She was tolerable to look at, despite her Hapsburg lip. She had "a queenly carriage," and queenly horses to pull it!

She liked to dress fashionably—a queen shouldn't look like a chambermaid! The French textile industry expected her to set high standards. It was her duty to dress extravagantly, so she spent a fortune on clothes, jewelry, earrings, diamonds, feathers, and costly fripperies. Her mother complained that her plumage made her look like an actress. Her feathered headdresses grew and grew, out of control. If they had continued unchecked, they would have necessitated a revolution in architecture. The bodies of carriages would have had to be enlarged to accommodate the ridiculous feathers. Her hats were big enough for ten heads. The queen became top-heavy. Her center-of-gravity rose to her brain. She had to put on her chemise from below.

The ridiculous feathers

She had more staff than a disabled person.[96] Tens of thousands of people served her royal court and her lounge lizards. Some were paid for doing nothing, but her mistress of the robes wore herself out making petticoat flounces, whatever they were. The queen's continual changes wreaked havoc on French fashion, causing great expense to aspirants to the middle class. One hundred twenty thousand livres a year were never enough, but what of it? Her silly old bills were rarely paid.

Lafayette said that the cost of one of her fetes would feed a regiment in America for a whole year. But Marie Antoinette didn't care about regiments in America. Told that her amusements were too conspicuous, she created

---

[96] Including a bed warmer. How would that look on a résumé?

very private pleasure gardens at Trianon. They were so private that even the king didn't go there without an invitation. But alas, the cost was not private. Not after the Red Book came out. It cost lots of money to give the queen's *hameau* the aspect of poverty and to keep the royal sheep and goats properly perfumed, as befitted their social importance.

Marie Antoinette got much good advice from her mother, who nagged her to do her duty and produce a male heir. After her mother's death in 1780, the fishwives of Paris picked up the slack, and the poets and balladeers didn't miss a thing. Marie Antoinette was kept well informed of her faults, but how could she do her duty if the king couldn't do his? He had a very private problem that we won't go into here.[97] Haslip says she was still a virgin after seven years of marriage. Whose fault was that? When the queen did finally deliver a child, it was a girl. Whose fault was that? In 1781 she finally delivered a male heir and the French people loved it. So far so good. No revolution in sight.

But meanwhile, her featherbrained pals were draining the treasury. It wasn't so much the feathers they wore, it was the way they feathered their nests. Tony frittered away a fortune on faro and horse racing, on real estate, landscaping, and gardening. Then, much to her surprise, the French treasury suddenly ran dry in 1786, its credit rating lower than a snake's. The cupboard was bare! The party was over! The piper had to be paid! Belts would have to be tightened. Yes, even royal belts! It wasn't all her fault. Benjamin Franklin diverted lots of French francs into the American Revolution and filled the heads of the French underclass with visions of *liberté, egalité, fraternité* and all that. The finance ministers shared the blame. They borrowed and borrowed for years, rather than tax the rich.

---

[97] He could aim his pistol but not shoot.

Before long, everybody was upset. The nobles and the church because of new taxes, idlers because they were sacked, the poor because there was no bread. After a poor harvest in 1788, the mood got nasty. Alas, Marie Antoinette's popularity was inversely linked to the price of bread. Never a good arrangement!

The queen had always had enemies, such as her many creditors, the Jacobin Party, and Madame du Barry, the previous king's playmate, known as "the Creature" or "the Whore." The king's aunts hated Austrians and didn't care who knew it. But now, suddenly, there were enemies everywhere. The queen became known as "Madame Deficit" or "the Austrian Whore" or "the Baker's Wife."[98]

Meanwhile, King Louie was not paying attention. Somnolent from obesity, he slept through dire warnings. No high school student ever dozed through more world history than did Louis XVI, and when he wasn't sleeping he was preoccupied with slaughtering deer in the Forest of Rambouillet. Deer, after all, were made out of meat. But Louie had to call the Estates General into session to deal with the financial crisis. The fun began when all three estates ganged up on the poor, hapless king. They all wanted a constitution. Louie stalled for time. He saw no need for a constitution written by uppity tramps in the Third Estate. God wanted *him* to rule, he insisted. God never said anything about a constitution. That was never part of the deal.

In 1789 Louie lost control and the Third Estate, or unwashed rabble, took over and ran amok. France became a hungrocracy—ruled by the hungry. Of course, King Louie claimed to be one of the hungry, but it was hard to take him seriously, encased as he was in all that blubber.

After two years of stalling Louie finally caved in and agreed to the infernal constitution, but gave the

---

[98] The king was suspected of hoarding grain at Versailles. He probably was too, the fat pig.

impression that his heart was not in it. Indeed, he was plotting with foreign royalists to invade France and put a stop to this wretched constitution business.

Imprisoned in the tower

The royals were imprisoned, to keep them out of trouble. Even then, thirty dressmakers worked incessantly for Marie Antoinette, whose need for petticoat flounces continued unabated. The family devoured beef and bacon, fish and fowl, as if they grew on trees. Nothing could spoil the king's appetite!

There were more complaints about Marie Antoinette, that she spoke French like a German and supported Austrian claims on Bavaria. That she was not sufficiently Frenchified. That she did not pay for her wedding. That she did not observe the ridiculous customs of the French court. That she did not invite the right people to her parties. That she degraded herself by talking to commoners. That she danced Scottish reels. That she spent too much money on jewelry. That she meddled in politics and wore the pants in her family. How could she not meddle in politics after Maurepas, the brains behind the king, died in 1781? How could she not wear the pants in the family after Louie outgrew them?

Marie Antoinette was not all bad. She threw good parties and gave good dinners. *Le Grand Couvert* was a good show. This was the observing, from balconies, of the royal couple at table. It was great fun watching the king wolf his food, as he was a world-class glutton. If you were lucky you might get to see them bombard each other with bread pellets. Well, it was something to tell your grandchildren about!

At her trial in 1793 she was charged with blood-sucking, arrogance, aloofness, pomp and glitter, frivolity, dissipation, extravagance, having sapphic tendencies, incest, corresponding with foreign powers such as her brother. No doubt she was guilty of some of these. The main charges against the king were: conspiring with foreign powers, unfair taxation, being a drip, hoarding food, and causing widespread famine by eating so much. Yes, he was guilty of some of these.

Louie and Tony should have agreed to step down. They could have taken up goat farming and lived happily ever after, but had no sense. He insisted that God wanted him to rule, all by himself. He needed God's permission to step down. Thanks for the offer, but no thanks. He didn't need any help from a constitution. He liked fat living—he didn't want to go hungry! And she didn't know how she could bear life without a throne. Where would she sit? How ever could she manage without her thousands of servants? So the National Convention abolished the monarchy in 1792. It remained only to abolish the monarchs. Louie's mouth—including his whole head— was severed from his stomach. They got hers too. Sorry about the ending. She only wanted to have fun. Was that so terrible? In attempting to preserve their privileges, Louie and Tony lost their heads, and their privileges too. So it was a bad bargain, and let it be a lesson to us all. They didn't leave much of a legacy: only a new crop of regicides.

Her life teaches us that if you must marry a dauphin that you have never even seen, first check an almanac to see if a revolution is due. Never allow your life expectancy to be indexed to the price of bread. And never, never swap your head for a throne. There is no future in it. Besides, modern lounge chairs are more comfortable than her old, moldy throne ever was. And a lot less trouble. Her old throne did not even recline!

You ask, what became of the sheepdog? It remained with her to the end. After that, frankly I don't give a damn.

Bismarck

Otto von Bismarck invented Germany. Before him it was just a petty assortment of petty principalities and petty dukedoms ruled by petty princes and petty dukes with petty intentions. Napoleon called it "these small and good-for-nothing states, powerless through their disunion." Bismarck made them into the big, bad, "Second Reich."

A Junker from Prussia, he misspent his youth brawling, partying, and smoking. His college years at Göttingen were unremarkable, except for that time when he ate 150 oysters at one sitting.[99] Known as "Mad Bismarck," he majored in beer drinking, dueling, eating, and carrying on. Some say it was only fencing he did, not really dueling. Then what about that time when he

---

[99] I'm not going to mention that Bismarck was born on All-Fool's Day. That would be a cheap shot.

challenged another student to a duel for laughing at his dog and refusing to apologize to it? Three paces with pistols, and no barrier. Was *that* fencing?[100]

And there were ladies of doubtful reputation. Horses and women couldn't be wild enough for young Bismarck, whose chief interests in life were wursts, roast meats, champagnes and wines, mushrooms, fish, and Erfurt beer. He believed that the purpose of life was to eat and drink, and vowed to consume five thousand bottles of champagne in his lifetime, in addition to wines, brandies, "Black Velvet," and plain booze. He got off to a running start.

The leading elements of his personality were misanthropy, bellicosity, intoxication, and of course, indigestion. He was fond of brooding, and worrying about his poor liver. Unable to tolerate social equals, he enjoyed the company of dogs and serfs. He liked being king of the hill. He thought it would be great fun to manage, risk, and mostly spend, other people's money, so he went into politics. Bismarck believed that raising corn was more worthwhile than politics, but he had a will-to-power, not a will-to-corn.

Dueling was not the only way to adjust differences. There was also diplomacy, the art of saying nothing in many words. But Bismarck's diplomatic skills extended beyond words. They included tears, hysterics, breaking door handles, smashing crockery, tantrums, threatening to jump from high windows, and threatening to go insane like Frederick William IV. He and Emperor William I liked to sob together, long before male bonding became fashionable.

Bismarck hated democracy, regarding it as an evil dragon to be slayed. He derived his authority from the king's divine right, as he had no right of his own, divine or

---

[100] The student finally apologized to Bismarck's dog, mainly in deference to the pistol on Bismarck's hip. I thought you'd want to know how it turned out.

otherwise. King William was easily hijacked. Bismarck became his lap dog—and his guard dog too, because William felt he needed protection from liberals. Bismarck had only to threaten to resign and the king would go into a panic, fearing that without Bismarck liberals would take over and democracy would break out and run amok through the palace, laying waste to everything. When his monarch went mad in 1857, did Bismarck ask himself whether monarchy was really such a good idea? Of course not! Frederick William had always been peculiar, but so are most people who think they have divine rights.

War was part of Bismarck's program, as peace was too boring. "Humanitarian rubbish," he called it, believing that issues should be decided by "blood and iron," though not by *his* blood or *his* iron. The trouble with war was that one might not win. Yet war seemed "the natural state of mankind," at least until his sons came of draft age. War was inevitable after all, just "enlarging our house according to our needs." And so he provoked three wars, blaming "God's inscrutable will," to enlarge Prussia's house.

Bismarck admitted that no one had attacked Prussia, but some of its neighbors had "ominously stood at attention" and you can't allow that! A nervous Nellie, he was terrified that the neighbors might be brazen enough to do what he was trying to do. The Industrial Revolution in the Ruhr Valley gave Prussia immense military advantages. Prussia had only to say "boo" to get its way, but saying "boo" would not unite the petty German states. There would still be obstacles:

> * King William did not want to be emperor of Germany; it didn't sound right. He enjoyed being king of Prussia and thought that would look better in the history books. Germany indeed! Besides, some of those petty German states contained Slavs, democrats, socialists, parliamentary bodies, and plain riffraff.

* The French did not like the idea of having a "Second Reich" next door. Would you?
* The Catholic South Germans did not want to take orders from Junker Protestants.
* The petty princes wanted to keep everything petty.
* As usual, the Austrians would not behave.

So Bismarck provoked three wars to overcome these obstacles and make the German states unite. Actually, to swallow them up into a bigger and better Prussia, because *Germany* meant Greater Prussia. Bismarck was not attached to names. About 1866 he started calling himself German, just for the record, but if you scratched him hard enough you'd still find a Prussian underneath. Call it whatever you like, he said, as long as it dominates Europe.

"Without me three great wars would not have happened and eighty thousand men would not have perished," Bismarck admitted. "Attila was a lamb compared with me." But he liked to point out that most of those men would "be dead anyhow forty years hence."[101] So it was OK. Besides, he had come to an agreement with God over those wars. Bismarck had no vision of a Europe living in peace and harmony. He preferred an all-powerful Prussia surrounded by weak, crippled, satellite states. The neighbors were weeds that needed to be thinned from time to time. Especially the French and the Austrians.

Bismarck resembled a Nordic god. He looked the archetypal Prussian officer, mounted on a huge horse, wearing a great cloak, with gleaming hawk eyes and a steel helmet. An impressive sight! Never mind that he was

---

[101] When he went hunting, Bismarck found himself unable to pull the trigger, "for I could see nothing but mothers and babies." But during the Franco-Prussian War, told that French women and children were starving, he replied, "Corpses need no shelter or food."

a draft dodger whose military experience mostly consisted of the three wars he started. Why bring that up? Unsuited to military discipline, he feigned a pain in his arm to avoid military service.[102] But he liked wearing the uniforms—he thought he looked dashing in them. And he liked to assume military airs, whatever they were.

Equating democracy with disorder, Bismarck promoted a strong monarchy and a weak Reichstag, thus enabling his successor, Kaiser Wilhelm II, to wreak havoc

---

[102] Later he complained that shaking hands made his hand hurt.

on the world unchecked. He did not often agree with Kaiser Willy, though they did have a few things in common—they both hated Willy's parents. Bismarck called the Reichstag "three hundred cabbageheads." They called him King Bismarck I. The trouble with the cabbageheads, he thought, was that they drank too much beer and not enough champagne. Beer caused democracy, though it didn't seem to work that way on him. In fact, Bismarck drank so much beer that it became fashionable in Berlin. Bavarian brewers gave him free beer by the barrel, so he drank it. What else can you do with free beer? Kill slugs? But all that free beer failed to make him a liberal democrat. Even beer has to have something to work with.

Bismarck was not interested in colonies, except those that spoke German. He wanted a linguistic union because he did not want to mess with barbaric foreign languages. However, he could see no harm in taking Alsace and Lorraine from the French and Schleswig and Holstein from the Danes and the Austrians. Weren't their inhabitants almost human enough to be German? And he wanted a religious union, feeling that Prussia should expand only as far as Protestantism extended, and then stop. Bismarck wanted the pope weak and crippled, like any other neighbor, and couldn't stand neighbors who claimed to be infallible. But he did not go to war with Italy, no doubt because of its barbaric language and religion.

You have probably heard that Bismarck was anti-Semitic. Yes, he hated Jews, but only because they were people, not because they were Jews. Is *that* still anti-Semitism?

Although he liked to call himself "God's chosen instrument," Bismarck did not believe in a conventional god. He believed in a kind of divine vice-regent in the sky. He made a deal with God, agreeing to believe in her if she satisfied certain conditions. It is not known whether God complied with the terms. Although he felt occasional outbursts of Christian feeling, Bismarck usually mistook them for lumbago. His wife Johanna was so pious that she wanted the godless French exterminated.

Bismarck is considered the founder of realpolitik, which makes it a principle not to have any principles. Unscrupulous, even for a politician, he kept his enemies guessing, and keeps historians guessing to this day. Don't expect to understand Bismarck unless you are a chess master, a sociopath, or both. He often disagreed with himself.

Bismarck tried to block democracy by starting his own newspaper, to spew his own propaganda far and wide. Karl Marx once refused to join its staff, believing he could do better. The liberal press helped make Bismarck the most hated man in Prussia, for a while, but his territorial acquisitions following his wars made him popular, as nothing succeeds like success. Nevermind the blood and gore, didn't he bring home the bacon to Prussia? Not to mention the Strasbourg geese? Bismarck is considered a genius because Prussia won the battle of Königgrätz (Sadowa) in 1866; if Prussia had lost he might have been hanged, thus rendering this chapter unnecessary.

He made lots of blunders, even some silly ones, but got away with most. Taking Alsace and Lorraine was a blunder, unless you think Strasbourg geese were worth a world war. Expelling thirty thousand Poles did not please the Russians, or the Poles either. His "blood and iron" speech was a tactical blunder. But his silliest blunder was thinking he could control Kaiser Wilhelm. Nobody could control Kaiser Willy.

Bismarck left many legacies, though Kaiser Willy undid most of them. He left a Second Reich, a German central bank, a strong monarchy in the hands of a weak-headed monarch, a resurgence in the social status of beer. He left a social welfare state, hoping to co-opt the socialists. He set the stage for World War I, which led to World War II, which led to . . .

Bismarck liked to boast that he had seen three kings naked, but you can see better any day on the Internet. How much was Bismarck worth? A Belgian boilermaker once offered to kill him for sixty thousand francs. Inflation would make him worth even more today.

In old age Bismarck became obsessed with insurance: social insurance, defensive alliances, protectionism, Doberman pinschers. He no longer wanted to create, only to preserve. When he grew too old to beat his peasants he retired to his Lauenburg estate, to dream in the woods with his best friends, his hounds. Ludwig said that Bismarck was more intimate with his dogs than with his wife.[103] He wanted to spend eternity with them in the great kennel in the sky. Bismarck's hounds were huge, highly-strung, ugly and stupid, but loyal, and he regarded them as cousins. "Hounds follow those who feed them," he observed.

Shooting was the best way to spend one's time, he said, believing he had been born to shoot. He enjoyed writing invective, but his favorite hobby was collecting, especially collecting grievances. He had an impressive collection of symptoms as well, including ulcers, indigestion, bloating, lumbago. These were known as "Bismarck's domestic problems." They came from eating and drinking too well. His enemies claimed he was full of wursts and Erfurt beer, and they were probably right.

Bismarck surfed the tide of the Industrial Revolution and managed to be dead before his chickens came to roost. His life teaches us that there is indeed something to be said for pettiness.

---

[103] Bismarck slept with his hounds. I don't know where his wife slept. It's really none of my business.

Queen Victoria

Victoria was an innocent young thing when she became queen of England. She didn't know what to do, so she relied on her prime ministers to make her mistakes for her. She did have political power, however, having such a genius for nagging her ministers and making a nuisance of herself that she became the most powerful fusspot in nineteenth century Britain. People feared her. The mighty Bismarck mopped his brow after an interview with her. In Africa she was known as "the Great White Queen who eats whole countries for breakfast." People watched for the "bad blood to come out" in her, the blood of her sadistic brute of a father, the Duke of Kent. She personified the British lion.

But in fact she was a dour-faced, timid little homebody with a social phobia. After her coronation in Westminster Abbey, amid ridiculous grandiosity, she rushed home to give her dog a bath! Her hands were soft, and she liked to hold them out to be kissed. But she was no softy. She could demolish people with one look. One disapproving nod, one royal "humbug," could shrivel the strongest man into a mere subject. Her motto was, "We are not amused."[104]

As an infant she was "as plump as a partridge." Later she became stout to the point of no return, and people thought they saw in her a remarkable resemblance to her grandfather—the one who went insane. They called her "Mad King George in petticoats." The queen liked to eat "soft, pappy foods." When she became a soft, pappy person her doctor put her on a diet, which she readily accepted, simply adding it to her already copious meals. Creevy said that she gobbled her food and showed too much gum.

Queen Victoria was a celebrated prude. When people called her hot-blooded or passionate, they were referring to her temper. She was against some bodily functions, believing that sex and pregnancy were not nice. Childbirth was so disgusting that she spoke of it only in German; it made her feel like a cow or a dog. She didn't much like babies, but somehow had nine of them.[105] This was believed to be the fault of Prince Albert, her husband. After all, his motto was, "Keep up your pecker." But some of her biographers claim that she debilitated poor Albert with her incessant amorous demands, so I can't say who was to blame for the nine children.

Babies were repulsive little animals, she thought, behaving more like frogs than people. They didn't become human until they were at least six months old. Some of

---

[104] The queen became so fat that she spoke of herself in the first person plural.

[105] Political crises were forbidden during her pregnancies.

her grandchildren took longer than that. They all had Coburg noses and weak chins. Like most babies, they looked like Winston Churchill for a while, but had no way of knowing it at the time.

Prince Albert was known as Albert the Perfect, Dearest Angel Albert, or Saint Albert. He was her prince charming, the most perfect being who ever lived, despite his receding hairline, Coburg nose, and portly middle. She could overlook his Coburg nose because she had a Hanover nose herself. She called him her "guardian angel." Has no one questioned the propriety of her having nine children by her guardian angel? Prince Albert was so good that there is some question whether he actually existed.[106] Was he just a spirit of benevolence? Then how would you explain the nine kids?

Dearest Albert did have faults, however, in addition to his Coburg nose. He was a shooting machine who liked to stalk and murder deer and practically everything else in the woods, even cute little grouse and endangered species.[107] He was a foreigner with a tendency to lapse into German, and he had difficulty digesting English food. But he is not the Prince Albert on the tobacco can. That is his grandson, Prince Albert Victor. Don't look for Dearest Albert on a can!

When Dearest Albert died in 1861, Queen Victoria went into history's longest depression, unsurpassed even by the Great Depression of the 1930s, and became a patroness of the arts. She decided that every village, every mere hamlet, in England desperately needed a magnificent monument to Dearest Albert, paid for out of the public purse. Finally, by the 1880s, with monuments cluttering the countryside far and wide, people had had enough of Dearest Albert and refused to give her any

---

[106] Even his pigs won prizes! Their manure was world-class.
[107] Capercaillies went extinct in Britain. Guess who was the first person to shoot them after they were reintroduced in 1837.

more money for statues. They thought it was high time for her to pull herself together. But she refused to accept Albert's death, becoming instead preoccupied with death, judgment, worms, corpses, cemeteries, and black clothing. It was said that black was her favorite color. Black was her *only* color! Attending a funeral was her idea of a good time. Grieving was good for her nerves, she insisted, as she mastered the art of morbidity. For forty years she continued to have Dearest Albert's clothes laid out each evening, with hot water and a clean towel. His chamber pot was scrubbed every morning, though he hardly ever used it.

In her mourning, the Queen was rarely seen in public, except to dedicate more statues of Dearest Albert. She complained of overwork and her royal "crown of thorns." When she didn't get her way, she would threaten to run away to Australia with her whole retinue. She hated liberals, especially Gladstone. But it is not true that she hated people, as she liked dead people. She also hated turtle soup, mutton, and brushing her teeth. She disliked being "in harness" but felt she had a vocation to do good, so she started a home for dogs in Battersea, and banned mutton at court. And she resolved to save England from democracy. She was demophobic.

Her foreign policy was simple: she was for the countries ruled by her relatives, and against those ruled by mere foreigners, especially the French. Related to most of the ruling houses of Europe, she generously shared with them her hemophilia.[108] She had no use for "little Englands," preferring a spirited foreign policy. "I fear wars will never cease," she complained. Could she help it that the Zulus were uppity, the Irish dreadful, the Russians and the French detestable? The Boers were "horrid people" because they would not let the English

---

[108] Her favorite therapies, rolling in the grass and washing her neck with vinegar, usually failed to cure it. Even barley soup didn't help.

take their gold. Peace with honor would be nice, of course, but she preferred peace with plunder. "There is no finer death for a man than on a battlefield." But she was against "wanton aggression" so she grabbed only nine million square miles of territory. This was "natural progression," not imperialism. She could not understand why colonial subjects didn't like the British. After all, she liked them fine! On a visit to Ireland, she noted that the Irish had a peculiar way of cheering, more like yelling or hooting. "Booing," she believed it was called.

For an overview of her domestic policies, see the novels of Charles Dickens. She believed that Dickensian slums were good enough for the poor, who should be generously provided with work, at least ten hours per day, but otherwise left alone, as public money was desperately needed for more monuments to Dearest Albert. Too much education was not good for the poor. It might get out of hand, causing England to "slide down" into democracy.

A constitutional monarch, she liked to flirt with her prime ministers, especially Disraeli, who flattered her shamelessly, intoxicating her with sugary language and thick slabs of adulation until she "glided about the room like a bird." A remarkable sight to see! His flattery was one of the few things that really did amuse her. She loved it when he likened her to Spenser's Faery Queen! He called her "the Faery"; she called him her "Primo." He sent her a valentine every year and kissed her fat little royal hand. She sent him primroses.[109] It would have been a fairy tale romance, but for the two people involved. It was Disraeli who made the queen a land grabber. Dearest Albert did not approve of imperialism, except for Ireland, which needed "an infusion of Protestants."

It was said that she had no feeling for Gladstone, despite his sixty-five years of loyal service to her. This is not true, as she loathed him with a passion approaching hysteria. She called him "that half-mad firebrand," that "dreadful man." He was "always reforming everything." And he spoke to her as if she were a "public meeting" or an institution. But she enjoyed bickering with him.

There were complaints about the queen, that she never did any work and should be replaced by a republic. Gladstone was forever nagging her to do something, something public, something visible, to earn her keep. Something that could be proven. But to hear her tell it, she was burdened beyond human limits by her "arduous duties." In fact, she *did* do something: she grabbed territory, lots of it. Or rather, her man Disraeli did.

Queen Victoria was not all bad. She once saved the life of a soldier in the Boer War. The box of chocolates she

---

[109] Every year, on the anniversary of Disraeli's death, countless pretty little primroses were brutally uprooted and heaped upon his grave.

gave her troops stopped a bullet for Private James Humphrey! And didn't she always pray for Fenians before having them hanged?

You needn't keep track of Queen Victoria's children, except maybe Poor Bertie.[110] Poor Bertie hung out with a fast set. He was too Hanover, not enough Coburg, for her taste. Mainly he was fat, vulgar, and stupid, and had deplorable habits, such as smoking, gaming, wenching, and associating with Americans and Jews. The queen also smoked, but only "to keep the midges away." She found Bohemians exotic, but not when Bertie did it. She had many grandchildren, as her children reproduced "like the rabbits in Windsor Park." None of them amounted to much, except Willy, the one who came to be known as "the Mad Dog of Europe." He was rapscallion enough to merit his own chapter in this book.

In 1878, Alexander Graham Bell gave the queen a telephone, the first one in England. She was not impressed with it because she could not find anyone to call up.

Queen Victoria enjoyed the little things in life: flattery, fidgeting, gossiping about the illnesses of others, matchmaking. Drinking beer and cussing. Flirting with her servant, John Brown, who had much in common with her, especially dourness. It was cute the way he ordered her about. But don't believe the rumors that she had an affair with John Bull.

She reigned gloriously over 350 million subjects, but did not actually govern. More a royal nuisance than a ruler, she mostly meddled in foreign and domestic affairs. Lytton Strachey said, "She was only dimly aware of what was happening." And Lady Strachey said, "The queen could not help being stupid, but she tried to do her duty." Always shy, Victoria felt uncomfortable in the presence of those more clever than she, which was practically everybody. In 1897, there was a big celebration to observe

---

[110] Not his baptism name.

her golden jubilee, sixty years of her meddling, but mostly that the empire had grown so big. Rudyard Kipling said that she owned "'alf of creation." She was the Grandmama of Europe.[111]

On her death bed, Queen Victoria asked for her dog Turi and then died, leaving thirty-seven grandchildren, two million quid sterling, Turi, widespread hemophilia, and sixty million words of memoir and correspondence. Poor Bertie destroyed most of her letters when he became King Edward VII. They reminded Lytton Strachey of a turned-on tap. Her journals were said to be "too prurient" and too revealing to be permitted to survive. Articles of the queen's underwear are occasionally available at auctions, but be prepared to pay high prices. Her bloomers sold for nine thousand dollars and probably would not even fit you.[112]

Queen Victoria is important because she was the first Victorian, in at the very beginning of the Victorian Age. Indeed, she became an adjective in her own lifetime. *Victorian* means bad in bed, uptight in morals, pompous and priggish in manner, overdone in architecture, and overstuffed in furniture. It is a handy word. Add it to your vocabulary.

Queen Victoria's life teaches us that if you are afraid of little old ladies, you are not alone.

---

[111] Her grandchildren called her "Gangan" because she looked like one to them.
[112] Unless you are built like a balloon, with a fifty inch waist.

V

Imperialist Warmongers

Hernan Cortes

Robert Clive

Napoleon Bonaparte

Cecil Rhodes

Hernan Cortes

Hernan Cortes had a sickness of the heart that only gold could cure, and then only for a while. That's why he was not satisfied with being a notary public. No desk job could contain him for long. He wanted to be where the gold was.

As a youth in Estremadura, he was given to quarreling, so decided to make a career of it. Why deny a natural aptitude? His parents wanted him to go away to seek his fortune—as far away as possible. They gave him money for his first transatlantic voyage, hoping to get rid of him. It worked, because by then it was common knowledge that the streets in America were paved with gold. Cortes wanted to go there, dig up a few streets, and ship them back to Spain to be melted down into gold bars. What was the harm in that? Offered land in Santo Domingo, he scorned farming. You can't grow gold!

The pope said the Spanish could have Mexico if they would convert the heathen natives to Christianity. But the Mexicans were already very religious—they were cannibals. They had an unpleasant habit of cutting out human hearts that were still in use, and calling it religion. Cortes tried to persuade them to eat the body of Christ instead of one another, but they would not agree to be converted, not after Cortes told them there would be Spaniards in heaven. Sure, their god Huitzilopochtli was a nuisance, with his insatiable demands for fresh human hearts, but Cortes was a nuisance too, and a bore. Besides, they like stewed thighs.

Mexicans were called Indians, although they were nowhere near India or Cleveland. They called themselves Aztecs, Toltecs, Mixtecs, etc., but to Cortes they were all low-techs, subhumans, children who needed to be spanked now and then.[113] Much like the Moors in Spain. Sure, they made nice art, but so did bees and spiders. They were obstinate and rebellious and refused to co-operate in their own subjugation. They had "evil designs," said Cortes, forgetting whose country he had invaded. He felt that Mexicans did not give gold the love and appreciation it deserved. They regarded it as excrement, albeit divine. Sure it was pretty, but so what? They preferred green jade. They were on a jade standard.

Mexicans didn't think much of Spaniards either, absurd beings who rode on the sea in floating castles and worshipped a pale goddess. They humbled themselves before wooden poles. Their faces were covered with hair. They smelled and tasted bad. They were forever asking for food, water, and gold, and casting down idols, and planting crosses that never even sprouted. They had a religious fixation on virgins.

Cortes had a communication problem with Mexicans because their Spanish was atrocious—they were not very

---

[113] The Totonacs believed that fish had once been people. This is ridiculous; only a few of them had been.

bright.[114] "¿Que pasa?" he would ask them, and they would just stand there looking perplexed. But Marina was bright, a local who could speak Mayan and Nahuatl. She soon picked up pidgin Spanish and was handy in translating. She was handy for other things as well—they had a baby to prove it—but Cortes ditched her when the romance went out of their relationship. He was a cad with women, but I would not call him a bigamist. He was a multimist. Marina was known as Malina or Malinche because Mexicans could not pronounce the letter r and finally gave up trying.

Cortes tried not to butcher women and children unless they deserved it, often chivalrously branding and enslaving them instead of killing them. Women were useful, after all, in breadmaking and other services. He said his Spanish wife, Catalina Suarez, died of "asthma." Maybe she did, maybe she didn't, but rumor had it that it was caused by his hands on her neck. By the way, how did her "asthma" break her necklace? There were disturbing rumors about Cortes, as well as disturbing facts, and much loose talk about sudden convenient deaths of people who had never been sick before. But let's not jump to conclusions!

You ask, how did Cortes manage to subdue so many Mexicans with such a small band of cutthroats? Mostly by luck and pluck. He fit the description of Quetzalcoatl, a god of fertility who was last seen disappearing into the eastern sea, vowing to return in a one reed year to re-establish his rule. By chance Cortes arrived in a one reed year. Darned if he wasn't Quetzal himself, thought the locals, back from the summit of the cosmos! Better be nice to him! After all, Quetzalcoatl was Huitzilopochtli's brother.

Modern historians believe that Cortes was not a god after all, not from the summit of the cosmos, just a notary

---

[114] One Mexican chief was given a gift of a dog but had it killed, thinking it was a rat.

public from Estremadura, but in those days, without benefit of hindsight, how could anyone be sure? After all, Spaniards had many attributes of gods: they seemed to be immune from the pox; they could fire lightning from the bellies of cannons; their arrival was preceded by strange events, such as tongues of fire in the sky; they gave the Mexicans pretty beads, the kind worn by the gods. But eventually the natives figured out that Spaniards were not gods after all because they did not excrete gold, as the gods did, and they died like mere mortals. Then one day the locals found a dead horse and discovered that even horses were mortal! Who would have believed it? They should have known that horses were not gods, because gods do not permit Spaniards to ride on their backs.

But Spaniards were superior beings anyway because they had horses, vicious dogs, cannons, steel armor, muskets and gunpowder, crossbows, arquebuses, the wheel, smallpox, and God on their side. Occasionally St. James[115] or St. Peter would show up in battle to help out. There were reports that they had centaurs. Maybe they did, maybe they didn't. They had lots of karma on their side too, in the form of Mexican allies who hated Aztecs for the same reason Americans hate the IRS: taxes.[116]

The Aztecs had no gunpowder; they had the zero, but what good was that in combat?[117] They had cotton armor, bows and arrows, rocks, slings, and Huitzilopochtli on their side. Their vitality was sapped, thought the Spaniards, by frequent bathing (they were as crazy as Moors about bathing). Even so, things went badly at times for Cortes and his gang, but he would not turn back because he was a fugitive from what was then believed to be justice. He couldn't go home without the gold.

---

[115] St. James was a veteran of the Moorish wars.
[116] At least the IRS doesn't take your children and eat them. Not yet anyway.
[117] Besides, the Spanish also had the zero.

The Spaniards were offered dog meat, rats, lake scum that tasted like cheese, and old women to eat, but still they hungered for gold, the excrement of the gods! There is no accounting for taste, thought the locals. The Tlaxcalans were generous with their food because they were planning to eat the Spaniards later, but some Mexicans refused to eat Spaniards, complaining that they tasted bitter, even when chocolate-covered or masked with *mole,* garlic, or chillies.

History tells us—even if we are too polite to ask—that Cortes' men smelled bad. Mexicans fumigated them with incense when they had to approach them, but what they really needed was a bath. Spaniards always taste better after a bath—don't ask me how I know. Aztec priests smelled worse than Spaniards, like dead dogs. They had messy jobs.

Although Cortes reluctantly accepted cannibals into his armies, his Spaniards were not cannibals.[118] Being civilized Christians, they fed their victims to their dogs and then ate the dogs. He insisted that his men behave like decent Christian cutthroats. Cohabiting with heathen women was strictly forbidden, for example, so the women were baptized before being doled out to Spaniards. In 1521 the pope absolved them all with papal bulls, just in case they might have done something sinful at some point. I'm not saying they did, mind you.

When Cortes met Montezuma, he thought him a nice enough guy, amiable, affable, gracious. It was regrettable that he liked to eat the flesh of young boys, but nobody is perfect. Could he help it that he was very religious? His favorite dish was stewed thighs with maize, squash, or chili. But Montezuma did not eat babies.[119] Let's give him some credit for that. Montezuma tried to co-operate. He tried to introduce Christianity into his religious practices,

---

[118] But Cortes sealed his ships with human fat, according to de Gomara.

[119] Not enough meat on them.

but there seemed to be no Christian way to remove human hearts that were still being used. There still isn't, to this day. But he tried. When studying the Conquest, one cannot help but notice that there are no good guys in this story! This is why it would not make a good Hollywood movie. Also, not much love interest. None, in fact.

When Montezuma asked him what were his intentions in Mexico, Cortes was tongue-tied. What could he say? If his intention was trade, why the cannons? He wanted to do some sight-seeing, that's all, and maybe save a few souls, install a few virgins here and there, and abolish an abomination or two. And relieve the locals of any divine droppings that might be cluttering their landscapes. He wanted to be helpful, that's all. He wanted peace in Mexico. Well okay, peace with tribute.

Cortes at first pretended to be Montezuma's pal. He thought he could conquer him by force of personality, but he had no personality. Montezuma loved Cortes, said Lopez de Gomara, but gave him gold, hoping he would go away. It didn't work. The more gold he gave him, the more he stayed. It was like feeding a cat to make it go away—it doesn't work.

When Cortes went to the coast on business, leaving Alvarado in charge, all hell broke loose. The pretense of friendship ended. It was bloody war from then on, ending in a long siege. Cortes believed that fighting was noble. Besides, it was the only thing he knew how to do. Retreating was shameful, except for the natives.

After the fall of Tenochtitlan, Cortes made "improvements." No more tribute was to be paid to those mean, nasty Aztecs, he said. From now on it was to be paid to him. Captives were to be enslaved, not eaten. It was more efficient, and more Christian. Cortes banned human sacrifice, on penalty of death.

But things turned sour again in Tenochtitlan and Cortes had to make an unscheduled departure one night. Okay, it was a retreat. In their haste the Spaniards lost most of their booty in the lake. Hundreds of them died filthy rich that night, loaded down with gold, which was never found. The king's share was seized by French pirates on its way to Spain. Not having sense enough to quit, Cortes regrouped and attacked again.

Was it all worth it? He did see some interesting sights but failed to abolish many abominations. I hear tell sodomy still goes on today. But there were spin-offs: he introduced horses, mules, vicious dogs, plaster virgins, cheap beef and pork, mestizos, more pronounceable place names, smallpox, measles, plague, the nail, the screw, the pulley, and the candle to Mexico, not necessarily in that order. It is not true that he introduced syphilis into Europe, as Columbus had beaten him to it.[120]

Cortes is considered a great man because he snuffed out a quarter of a million lives. Only a great man could do that. Las Casas puts the death toll into the millions, but Cortes was not great enough to do that many all by himself. The human population plummeted and was replaced by pigs, dogs, cattle, horses, and Spaniards. This was known as modernizing Mexico. I suppose we have to give Cortes some credit for ending human sacrifice in Mexico, but don't you think the locals would eventually have figured out by themselves that the sun would still rise without the bloody offerings?

Of course there were complaints about the rotting corpses, the famines, and the Spanish Inquisition, which soon followed. Cortes was himself a self-appointed Inquisitor, using unchristian methods to force bastardized Christianity upon people who did not want it. His methods were blots on the history of the Conquest, which was itself a blot. Today there are no public monuments to Cortes in Mexico City, not even a public restroom. Some Mexicans are still sore about him, and still waiting for the real Quetzalcoatl to return. In Guatemala, Cortes forced

---

[120] The Spanish got syphilis and the Mexicans got smallpox, so it was an even exchange. A pox for a pox.

the natives to break up their idols and accept Christianity, but after he left they worshipped instead a lame horse he had left behind. A century later, their descendants were still worshipping horse idols. What can you do with such people?

Tenochtitlan was the most beautiful city in the world, said Cortes, sentimentally. At least it was the most beautiful city he ever destroyed. The Spanish renamed it Mexico City because they couldn't pronounce or spell Tenochtitlan, as who can? Cortes is credited with founding the city of Veracruz because he built a pillory and a gallows on the site.

Cortes had a beak nose, a humpback, a pinhead, bowed legs, a bulging forehead, a pigeon breast—he didn't look much like a god.[121] Of course he might have looked better four hundred years earlier, when he was alive, but his corpse looked awful when it was discovered in a wall in 1946. He died in Spain, but his bones were moved to Mexico, in accordance with his will, where he believed they would do more good. The wonder is that he died in bed with his heart still in his chest.

Cortes messed around with Montezuma's daughters and had at least one child by them. Was that taking imperialism a bit too far? Do you think less of him as the son-in-law of a cannibal? Cortes made lots of history, but could have made more money as a notary public. He could have been a darn good *notario*, but he had too much audacity and too little sense. His life teaches us to stay close to our desks and never go to sea because a peseta in the hand is worth two pesos in the bush.

---

[121] Cortes probably resembled a serpent, because *coatl* meant serpent in Nahuatl.

Robert Clive

Robert Clive went to India in 1744 to make money, not war. Commerce was the proper sphere and whole aim of his countrymen, he said, as he rampaged the countryside.

He started out at five quid a year in Madras, working for the Right Honourable East India Company, but wasn't satisfied with that. Who ever made a career out of five quid a year? he asked, rhetorically. Not content to be a harmless drudge, Clive enlisted in the company army. He was of a martial disposition anyway, and there was money in soldiering—more than five quid. They say he had "leadership qualities." You could call it that. Or you could call it brutality. Fighting the French got "warm" at times but he had no fear in battle, believing he had been born to be hanged. Providence was saving him for some special purpose, something good for more than five quid.

There was never any shortage of bogeymen to chase away, whether they were French "frogeaters" or Dutch "butterboxes" or Abdali the Afghan or Maratha pirates or Gazoody Khan. Clive chased them all away, for fun and profit. Then providence appointed him steward, a job that offered temptations, and by 1753 he was worth forty thousand quid. Clive liked temptations. He knew what to do with them.

He could now afford to get married—or frequent public women. His inordinate erectability was like to that of the apes, said Dr. Ives. But Clive's amorous exploits and venereal victories may be a bit exaggerated because in time opium weakened his works. "Opium has unmanned me," he complained in 1765. Indeed, by that time his unruly member had become "a nerveless droop." But in his salad days, Clive learned to smoke a hookah and enjoyed the fleshpots of Madras, at least until Margaret Maskelyne arrived from England in 1752, looking for Mr. Right. They were married, despite her big nose and her cats. For years after, Clive would moan about his miserable life, "ever since the year 1752." But something else might have happened in 1752 to make him miserable, something besides Margaret. We just don't know what it was.

After honeymooning in England, Clive was assigned to Fort St. David, a backwater near Madras, as deputy governor. It would have been a tedious assignment, as peace had been declared with the French, but the young nawab of Bengal got uppity and grabbed Calcutta, so Clive went to Bengal to adjust his regime a little and grab it back. Soon the young nawab was very dead, replaced by a nicer one, but the regime change destabilized the region so much that only a dictator could control it. So Clive became a dictator. The locals were full of trickery, he said; Indian nawabs had to be replaced by English nabobs. About that time national armies took over from company armies and the wars took on a nastiness not known before, except to the corpses. There could be no peace, said Clive, while there was one Frenchman in arms. The

French felt the same about Englishmen in arms. No one thought to ask the locals how they felt.

The moguls had little effective power after 1739, when raiders stole their Peacock Throne and created a nice power vacuum for Clive to step into, but he liked to drop them a few rupees now and then, just to keep them quiet. He liked having real moguls around as lackeys. The new nawab of Bengal got an allowance from Clive, to spend on hemp and dancing girls, so he was happy.

Clive was incorruptible, according to Clive, who was astonished at his moderation after the battle of Plassey in 1757, when he took not one rupee from the defeated nawab's purse, not even a little one that no one would have missed. But despite such exemplary honesty, Clive suddenly became very wealthy about that time, worth 234,000 quid, as the new puppet nawab paid him off. The English liked regime changes because of the payoffs.

By 1759, Clive was tired of fighting, but there was no longer any need for it. Thought to be invincible, he had only to say "boo" to send adversaries fleeing for their lives. Everybody was afraid of him. "We are employed in bullying and keeping under the black fellows," he wrote home. He had his own personal black fellow to keep under, a slave called Black Robin.

When Clive had amassed enough plunder to buy an English baronetcy, he and Margaret decided to return to England to bask in glory, maybe rest on a seat in Parliament, and cash in their kudos for gold before they got stale. They wanted to join the English snobocracy. But another bogeyman appeared, the Shah Zada, wayward son of a mogul. As a reward for chasing him away, Clive was granted a *jagir* worth thirty thousand quid a year— for life—from the new puppet nawab of Bengal. Known to historians as "the infamous *jagir*," this was a perk of office, an office that Clive had no intention of fulfilling, as he was already packing his bags for England. After all, he was a quid millionaire, wealthy enough to live in style in England. Five quid a year, indeed! Clive was now a real nabob. He had come a long way from his youth, when he had been "Rogue Bob" or "Idiot Bob." Clive was a pig in clover, said Samuel Johnson.

So he departed in 1760, leaving the Bengali exchequer bankrupt. Thinking he was finished with India forever, Clive took his hounds with him, his money, and even his wife.[122] He left his chickens behind, because they came home to roost as soon as he left. The Indian stables became so Augean with corruption that he had to return in 1765 to clean house. The trouble with corruption was that company servants were exploiting the same people

---

[122] But they left their infant son behind.

that the rt. honourable company wanted to exploit. So Clive abolished bribes and presents, except for his own infamous *jagir*. Clive felt that he deserved corruption. Hadn't he earned it? Company servants argued that they needed corruption to maintain their dignity. Dignity was expensive! After all, they were white men and expected to live like the nabobs they thought they were. But Clive ordered that corruption be reserved for those who had earned it, and he would be the judge of that.

Clive disagreed with Lawrence Sulivan,[123] a director of the rt. honourable company, who wanted him to stick to business and leave empire building alone. Sulivan wanted commercial advantages for the company—dividends, not dominions; Clive wanted to "go forward," as far as he could get. Having outgrown the rt. honourable company, he wanted it all. Besides, he had left a gaping hole in the Indian government that somebody had to fill. So he stepped over the line between business and empire and soon vast hordes of Englishmen were arriving in India, hoping to be miraculously converted into nabobs. Clive felt that there were already enough nabobs in India and they didn't need any more. Fortunes should be reserved for those with seniority, he said, about as much of it as he had.

Clive's "Dual System" meant that the natives got to collect the taxes and the English got to spend them. The puppet nawab was supposed to look after the interests of the Indian people. As he was a cipher with no power or money, the Indian people did not get looked after very well but, no matter, Clive prospered and bought more stock in the rt. honourable company.

You may have heard that Clive squeezed taxes out of poor peasants. Well, it is not true! He squeezed the *zemindars;* they squeezed the peasants. You have probably heard that Clive was cruel to the Indians. It is true that he threatened to cut off the ears of the vendors

---

[123] Did somebody knock the *l* out of him?

at Patna if they sold booze to his troops, but did you ever see him actually do it? Some English officers were known to shoot mutineers from guns, like Quaker Oats, but again, did you ever see Clive do it? That's what I thought! Meanwhile, the Black Hole of Calcutta was available for enforcing discipline; wasn't that what it was for? And flogging was perfectly legal until 1868.

By 1767 the English controlled India with an iron fist. Actually, two fists, as Clive was a two-fisted man. All was in perfect harmony, said Clive, as he drained India to the very dregs. Two years later a monstrous famine killed ten million Indians but don't blame it on Clive, who was nowhere near at the time.[124] He was back home in England, resting on his laurels. The famine was not his idea at all, as it was not good for business or empire. But he was finished with India, except that his infamous *jagir* came from there.

Clive wanted to be popular in England. He wanted to cut a figure in society, though he was a boor with no social graces. Sure, he was a whiz at soldier talk, but after that the conversation lagged. On the dance floor he had two left feet. The English felt they owed him nothing, not even kudos, since he had already helped himself. Never mind that he had once been the uncrowned king of India; he was not royalty in England.

Clive was a military genius, according to Clive, superior even to Hernan Cortes, because didn't he lick real white people, not just naked savages? In fact, Clive's military reputation might be a tad stretched. After all, wasn't it a drunken sailor named Strahan who captured Calcutta, all by himself? Wasn't Clive rescued by pirates at the siege of Arcot? At Plassey, wasn't the battle decided while Clive was attending to his wardrobe? Weren't the Dutch routed while Clive was playing whist? Didn't Hector Munro take the valley of the Ganges while Clive

---

[124] The English raised taxes during the famine. It didn't help much.

was in Brazil? Weren't the French ousted by Watson and Coote? Yes, but Clive had no peer at flattery, empty promises, bribery, forgery, rumor mongering, or plain deviousness.

There are soreheads who say that Clive was not as moral as he should have been, that history would have been nicer if the rod had not been spared in his childhood. It is true that he did sometimes play cards on the Sabbath, I won't deny it, but was it his fault that the times did not offer scope to the development of high moral character?

In Parliament there were mumblings and grumblings and even snarlings about Clive's infamous *jagir,* because it came out of rents that the rt. honourable company had to pay. Clive was the company's landlord! So in 1772 a Parliamentary committee enquired into Clive, just in case he might have done something improper. Indeed he had! The committee found Clive guilty of high crimes, but didn't those crimes promote the eternal glory of England? His "shocking enormities" stank to high heaven, but doesn't conquest create its own morality? Alas, no honest person could be found to convict him. The starving people of India were not invited to the enquiry. Clive was interrogated as if he were a sheep stealer, but in the end he didn't have to give back the sheep. Clive had presented his country with an empire, much as a cat presents its master with a dead bird, and his country wasn't sure at first what to do with it. But in time it decided to keep it, and the rest is history.

The English didn't really mean it. They were only trying to create a secure foundation for trade. They were as surprised as anyone when they discovered one afternoon at tea time that they had conquered an empire, in spite of themselves! Indeed, India proved to be too big for the rt. honourable company to handle; the English Crown had to step in and take over. By that time Clive was spent and finished with India. Leave the administering to others, he thought, not in the mood to administer tens of millions of starving people.

Warren Hastings and others continued where Clive left off. There were wars and more wars, it was a bloody mess. They had to do it all over, again and again, with fresh corpses on all sides, but in due time the English subjugated India, to prevent the sun from setting on the British Empire.

Robert Clive made a career of chasing people away. Indeed, it is a handy skill to have. While the groans of India mounted to the heavens, he became the wealthiest citizen in Britain. He took the money and ran, but his honor was heavily mortgaged, as he was not always up-to-date on ethical standards. The flexibility of his conscience was truly remarkable. He believed that two evils made a good—or at least a profit. They say he died from the weight of his own iniquities, but it was probably gallstones.

Napoleon Bonaparte

Napoleon is a puzzle to psychiatrists because he was the first person with a Napoleonic complex who really was Napoleon. As a child he was small and Corsican, so of course the other kids picked on him and kicked his shins. He went to military school to learn how to get even.

Napoleon despised the French—even more than was normal—but joined their army anyway, because he needed a job.[125] When revolution broke out in 1789 he sided with the unwashed rabble against the aristocrats. Not that he had any love for the rabble, but aristos were in his way, especially kings. He was against aristos until he became

---

[125] When did Napoleon become French? Never!

one. The bloodbath created job openings in the Republican army, allowing him to rise rapidly in the ranks.

The Battle of Toulon in 1793 was a Pyrrhic victory because he was wounded in the thigh and caught scabies. But it was good enough for a promotion to brigadier general, and soon he was getting even all over Europe, which was ruled by blue-blooded monarchs who took a dim view of revolutions and red-blooded Corsican runts. About this time Napoleon discovered that if you kill people, most of the time they will let you take their money. Much of history has been predicated on this observation. In 1795 General Bonaparte put down a revolt in Paris, thus becoming the toast of that city. The battle of Lodi in Italy was good for another promotion, to man of destiny. After Lodi, he could hear the patter of destiny's footsteps behind him.

But those infernal Brits were in his way, especially on the seas. Britannia ruled the waves, and didn't he know it? Napoleon thought England should be just another French island, like Corsica, a nation of harmless shopkeepers. Uppity Britain desperately needed to be invaded, he decided, but its mighty navy was an issue so he invaded Europe instead, and then Egypt. His Egyptian campaign did not work out, but how were the French people to know that? Did they have Internet access? He propagandized it into a glorious victory and by 1802 was consul for life. There is nothing like propaganda to give a loser the smell of victory. His newspaper dispatches from the front were the origins of the proverbial "to lie like a bulletin" and pretty soon everybody was talking about Napoleon, the invincible one, who could kick butt without ever getting kicked back. He never claimed to be particularly truthful. No one would have believed him if he had because he cheated shamelessly at whist and told fibs whenever he pleased.

Napoleon believed that the purpose of life was to keep acquiring more and more money, power, and glory, by whatever means. To extend one's dominion far and wide—

as far as India would be nice. He hated to see a throne going to waste. "Whenever I see an empty throne," he said, "I feel the urge to sit down on it!" And why not? In 1804 he saw his chance and crowned himself emperor of France, thus becoming Europe's first red-blooded, bourgeois monarch. But his court was hardly bourgeois. It was so regal that people couldn't help but ask, wasn't there some sort of revolution a few years back? Did it do any good? Does a mere bourgeois really need a grand master of the hounds? So much for *liberté, egalité, fraternité* and all that. Aristocracy was oozing back in, through ever-widening cracks in the French Revolution. Napoleon was getting uppity! His blood was turning blue!

The crowned heads of Europe were not impressed by his newfangled credentials, so he had to keep fighting, to get some respect. To "keep his glory warm," he said, as glory is not much use at room temperature. He was addicted to glory, which came from butchering other human beings. Where else? It didn't grow on trees.

Napoleon had divine right, like the crowned heads, according to the imperial catechism of 1806.[126] We don't know what kind of deal he made with God, but God was not much help to him in Spain or in Russia, and certainly not at Waterloo. Napoleon should have read the fine print.

In 1796, Napoleon married Josephine de Beauharnais, a widow with two children of dubious paternity. The Bonaparte family thought she was too dissolute to be a Bonaparte, but so was he. All things considered, she was about right for him. He had a low opinion of women anyway, and often said so, but believed they made the best wives. For him the heart was not the organ of sentiment; he felt emotion below the waist. He believed that women were for making babies and for knitting. Love is harmful to society, he said. "Nature intended women to be our slaves." Napoleon was sort of an anti-hippie who believed in making war, not love.

---

[126] Which was devised by Napoleon himself.

Nevertheless he was hopelessly besotted with Josephine. Some said it was her vacuous presence, her shallowness of mind, that appealed to him. Others that she had "the sweetest bottom in the world."[127] We may never know for sure what it was. Despite her sweet backside, Josephine was not the ideal wife. Her favorite hobby was spending his money. Her powers of weeping[128] have become legendary. She had a very possessive dog named Fortune, which refused to allow Napoleon into her bed on their wedding night. Fortune set territorial limits by biting Napoleon on the leg, so they had to work out a

---

[127] The other Bonapartes failed to appreciate Josephine's bottom.

[128] Fournier said that Napoleon was himself given to convulsive weeping. But is mutual weeping a solid foundation for a marriage?

time-share. Josephine had a chimpanzee that wore a frock and ate at table with a knife and fork. It took Napoleon's place when he was away on campaigns. Josephine chose swans as her emblem because they mated for life, but she mated whenever she pleased, and so did he.

But Napoleon needed Josephine. He even agreed to take her to war with him if she promised not to have her migraines. He was not the ideal husband either, as he had "funny little ways." He liked to display affection by pinching ears and slapping people around, and he had an unfortunate habit of ripping clothes off of women if they (the clothes) were of British manufacture. This would be politically incorrect today. His table manners also fell short of perfection, as he wolfed his food and sopped his bread in his gravy. When served crepinettes of partridge he would overturn the table every time. He liked to express himself by breaking furniture, throwing tantrums or crockery, and shooting Josephine's pet birds.

Napoleon came from a large family. His mother Letitia[129] insisted that his good fortune would not last. She refused to give up her day job, even when her sons were kings of Spain, Holland, Westphalia, etc. She was right. Killing people can be lucrative, but it's not steady. Sure enough, Napoleon's fortunes reversed. Spain became a costly quagmire, European coalitions formed against him, taxes went up, his popularity down. His continental blockade was meant to destroy Britain's economy, but it raised coffee and sugar prices in France. Alienating caffeine and sugar freaks is not a smart policy. His kidnapping the pope and holding him prisoner for years did not make him popular with Catholics. He really shouldn't have done it. Napoleon was forever bickering with the pope over who was boss. Was the church in the state or the state in the church? He thought the pope should render unto Caesar. The pope thought Napoleon

---

[129] Contrary to popular rumor, Letitia Bonaparte was never married to the Man in the Iron Mask.

was not Caesar and should let him go home. By 1809 Napoleon was so unpopular that destiny bailed out—God too—and he was on his own.

"Victory will bring us bread," said Napoleon to his hungry troops, forgetting where bread came from. He couldn't seem to leave well enough alone, always trying to improve everything he saw with a whiff of grapeshot[130] or a bayonet thrust. At least he was not stupid. In fact, he was a genius; he could do almost anything—except smile or laugh. They say he could seize ideas "by the arse," a lost art. Only a genius could make such a mess in so short a time. But sometimes he did stupid things, like invade Russia. Sensible people don't invade Russia. But Napoleon met his Waterloo at . . . well, at Waterloo. No amount of propaganda could make Waterloo a victory. It was straight downhill from then on.

Josephine could knit but could not make babies, or so it seemed, so Napoleon divorced her and married Marie Louise of Austria, a silly goose with a Hapsburg lip, but not without talent, as she could wiggle her ears. Marie Louise was believed to have other talents as well, such as the ability to keep her Austrian kinfolk quiet and the ability to produce a male heir. Marie Louise was a blueblood. By marrying her Napoleon became official nephew-in-law to King Louie XVI, which further dismayed fans of the Revolution of '89. It was his final break from the republican rabble. He named their son the King of Rome because he thought it would be great fun to spank a king. You wouldn't want Napoleon for a parent.

When Napoleon's fortunes reversed, Marie Louise went home to Austria. She was afraid of him anyway, as who wouldn't be? She had a nervous habit of crossing herself, out of fear, whenever she heard his name. This can put a strain on a marriage. But Napoleon had many mistresses when away from home on business. Mademoiselle Georges, for example, must have been good

---

[130] Or a whiff of propaganda.

in bed because he once blacked out while mating with her.[131] She didn't know what to make of it. He had a harem too, of young ladies of the palace. Some say he even messed around with Josephine's niece Stephanie, but let's not get into that!

Before he had finished getting even, Napoleon was exiled to the remote island of St. Helena, where it was hoped he would behave himself, assisted by three thousand British troops. He lived in a rat-infested house and passed his time dictating his memoirs, bickering with his British captors, groaning sublimely, and muttering "Bah!" He also spent a lot of time moping, and regretting that he had not hanged or shot the right people. Supremely bored, he was reduced to shooting goats[132] for amusement—he who had once shot Englishmen! In time he became as fat and round as a china pig. Having drained life to its dregs, he died on St. Helena, after giving orders to his doctor to pickle his heart in spirits of wine and take it to Marie Louise. She was not interested, nor was her new husband.

"Let us destroy England," said Napoleon, who failed to do so. It is still there, as we go to press. In fact, he left Great Britain greater than ever. He left Prussia militarized and itching for revenge. But he was not a total loser. Most historians agree that he succeeded at getting even, and then some. He also introduced the potato to the island of Elba and doubled the size of the United States by selling Louisiana. Millions of children did their homework out of fear that "Boney" would get them if they didn't. Known as Boney the Bugbear or the Boneyman, Napoleon later became the bogeyman that we knew so well as children.

Not that he hadn't been called worse. His old nurse from Corsica used to call him Figlio. He didn't mind that

---

[131] She claimed to have done the Duke of Wellington as well. She didn't like to take sides.

[132] The rats were too fast for him.

so much, but people who called him Puss-in-Boots were living very dangerously.

He left many legacies: the Napoleonic legend, the Napoleonic law code, the Napoleonic complex, triumphal arches, obsolete maps, the science of Egyptology, and millions of dead people (who would probably be dead by now anyway). Napoleon created more tragedies than Shakespeare did. More movies have been made about Napoleon than about Joan of Arc, Abraham Lincoln, and Alf Landon combined. Almost as many as about Bugs Bunny. Still, it was a shame that he did not do something useful.

The French painter Ingres painted Napoleon in a chariot, being escorted into heaven by angels. But Thomas Jefferson thought Napoleon went to the other place, calling him a "wretch" who caused "more misery and suffering to the world than any other being who ever lived before him." Well, at least he didn't bring scandal upon his family like his shameless sister Pauline, who posed for the sculptor Canova without a stitch on!

Napoleon fought sixty battles, without learning a thing. His imperial overreach ended as it always does. When will they ever learn? His life teaches us never to kick the shins of little children.

Cecil Rhodes

Cecil Rhodes wanted the whole world to be English. He loved England, although not enough to stay there.[133] He left to seek his fortune, and any other fortunes that were not being carefully watched. Upon arriving in South Africa, he decided it was good enough to be English, then succumbed to "diamond fever," a type of greed that was epidemic at the time. Alas, the poor man never recovered.

At Kimberley, known as "the Great Hole" (because that's what it was), he became a diamond miner, if you can call him that—the natives did all the work. He

---

[133] Some have called him "excessively English" but that seems unfair, as he detested cold mutton.

discovered that if he fed them mealie porridge and hit them now and then they would "work like niggers" for him.[134] That's what he called them, "black niggers" or "boys." Unfortunately, what they called him has been lost to history.[135]

The natives who worked for Rhodes did not wear any clothes because he didn't like pockets, or anywhere else where diamonds could be secretly stashed, for future reference, out of his sight. If you are wondering where they kept their snuff, they kept it in little boxes suspended from their ear lobes. Rhodes enjoyed having "a lot of black niggers to do what you like with."

"We are hard at work," he wrote home. It was hard work watching so many "boys" working. Then he got lucky. After cornering the DeBeers mine he cornered Barney Barnato, who had cornered the Kimberley mine. When he had cornered the whole bloody diamond industry, he adjusted the price of diamonds upward. Then came the profits, pouring in like the Johnstown flood. Soon he was no longer financially dependent upon his Aunt Sophy and his brother Frank. In fact, he was immensely wealthy!

What was a simple-living bachelor to do with all that money? He decided to spend it on his hobby: painting Africa red. That is, making it English. There was a desperate shortage of English people in Africa in those days, and the natives were so backward they didn't know a fish from a chip! It was simply the duty of the English to civilize Africa, and anything else they could get their hands on, before somebody else did.

Then Rhodes succumbed to another fever—gold fever. There was gold in the hinterland, he could almost smell it, so he had a fancy for going north. He believed

---

[134] Sorry but it is not possible to write about Rhodes without using the "n" word; it was his favorite word.
[135] Lobengula, king of the Matabeles, called Rhodes "Ulodzi," but we don't know whether this was a name or a cuss word.

that the hinterland was empty of people. Actually it was full of Africans, but it was hard to see them because they were not the right color to show up well. It was gold he was looking for, not black natives. He had no trouble seeing gold, even when it wasn't there.

He did eventually notice the natives, when they started shooting at him, and tried to purchase their land fair and square. If they wouldn't sell he tried "moral suasion." If that also failed he tried immoral suasion—cheating them out of it or scaring them with stories of the Great White Queen (Victoria) who ate whole countries for breakfast.[136] If that didn't work, he tried bribing them with rifles and gunboats.[137] Then, finally, he sent in the militia.

Lobengula was patronized, cajoled, bribed, bullied, hoodwinked, bamboozled, but mostly tricked, until he agreed to let ten white men dig a "big hole" on his land to look for gold. "Ten white men," he said, emphatically. They came by the thousands, their hearts full of pride, their bellies full of whiskey (the water wasn't safe to drink). What could poor Lobengula do about it? He put his gold in the road and ran away, another victim of destiny. Can nothing be done about destiny? His land became "Rhodesia." Add it to the British Empire.

Africans were not much more than monkeys, said Anthony Trollope. Barbarous heathens who needed someone to civilize them, or at least put trousers on them. Rhodes disagreed, arguing that the locals were human, although not nearly as human as the English. Sure they were in the way, but Rhodes did not want war. A man of peace, he wanted to get rid of the natives peacefully. This was not easily done, as the natives did not want to be got rid of. So there was war, white people being what they

---

[136] Lobengula had doubts about the existence of Queen Victoria, but I believe in her and you should too.
[137] It was illegal to arm savages, but maybe Lobengula liked to shoot at beer cans. Besides, the guns were obsolete.

were. Rhodes felt that the English were more human than Africans because they had Maxim guns.

After they had slaughtered the natives, it was time for the whites to slaughter one another, for the land was full of gold, diamonds, whiskey, avarice, and fortune hunters. Rhodes wanted to get along with the Boers; after all, they were white people. But most of the gold seemed to be on the Boer side of the border, in the Transvaal. The English wanted it and the Boers wouldn't let them have it, so war became inevitable.

Rhodes's doctor had no cure for gold fever. In fact, he fell victim to it himself. His hare-brained invasion of the Transvaal was a product of greed, reckless courage, good whiskey, and too little sense. It failed miserably, and inspired Africans to rise in rebellion. Rhodes tried to pretend that he hadn't ordered Dr. Jim's silly raid, but when he went to England he was scolded by the House of Commons for meddling in the affairs of too many countries. A few would have been enough, the Commons felt.

When war broke out with the Boers, the Mayor of Kimberley telegraphed Rhodes not to come, as he would bring danger to the town. Rhodes arrived just in time for the siege. Unable to get along with the military command at Kimberley, he seemed to think he owned the place. As a matter of fact, he did! He called it his "bread and cheese." Nevertheless, food became scarce during the siege. Rhodes tried to send the natives home, but they came running back, complaining that Boers were shooting at them. They had to be satisfied with horse-bone soup, mangel-wurzel, and scurvy, for the duration. Bread and cheese, indeed! Every day the *soup du jour* was the same old "siege soup." Eventually the long siege became serious, when Rhodes's private stash of champagnes and gourmet foods threatened depletion.

The war became a nuisance and Rhodes bored of it (no pun intended). He didn't like war; it was inconvenient. He preferred to "square" his enemies into submission, but the Boers scorned his bribes. What can you do with such people? The British finally won the war and the Transvaal became a modern, civilized place, with taxes, pollution, high cholesterol, fish and chips, and of course, trousers. As a consolation prize, the Boers got the war named after them. Rhodes wanted to end all wars forever with a universal Pax Brittanica, enforced by Maxim guns. But for some reason, it did not work out.

At the siege of Kimberley

Rhodes became prime minister of the British Cape Colony,[138] but his ministry was not always popular. Liberals objected to his "Strop Bill," also known as the

---

[138] He would have been the lord high-everything if Dr. Jim's silly raid had succeeded.

"Every Man to Wallop His Own Nigger Bill." It would have legalized flogging of the natives, but only for serious crimes, such as doing what white people did. You are no doubt wondering, where did Rhodes stand on sheep-dipping? Well, he was for it, but against double-dipping. Once was enough.

Civilized people, according to Rhodes, were those who could write their names and wipe their noses. They could write *his* name on ballots. They paid hut taxes and did not drop their aitches. But he was not among those who wanted to put trousers on the natives—trousers have pockets.

Rhodes was a loner. He did not fancy women, so naturally he became the world's most eligible bachelor. Sometimes he would go dancing, but just for the exercise. He was not interested in making babies, not even English babies. Some say he hated women, but he would never admit to it, at least not to Queen Victoria. Mainly he just didn't want them "fussing about." (Men hardly ever "fuss about.") Women saw him as a challenge—that he was, indeed. They mailed him proposals of marriage and plotted to catch him, but to no avail. He would not even hire female servants. Instead he liked to surround himself with big, blond, virile young men. He liked everything "big and simple." Besides, he claimed he already had a wife. Her name was Rhodesia. She was a red hot mama who kept him very busy!

Princess Radziwill became a problem. Rhodes had to keep a servant on the lookout for her. When she came he would dart out the back door and hide until he got the all-clear that she was gone. He was afraid of snakes, lions, ghosts, and marriage, but most of all of being alone with Princess Radziwill.[139]

Rhodes loved nature and was never happier than when slaughtering it on the veld. He had many other hobbies: writing wills, painting Africa red, annexing

---

[139] But Kaiser Wilhelm fancied Princess Radziwill.

territory, Johnny Grimmer, compounding natives, Neville Pickering, experimental farms, playing hide-and-seek with Princess Radziwill. But imperialism was his favorite hobby. He never cared for collecting butterflies or stamps. He preferred collecting other people's property. Imperialism is much like musical chairs. Everybody and his brother were trying to colonize Africa and Rhodes did not want to be the odd man out. He believed that Africa was his birthright. The Boers thought it was theirs. The Germans and the Portuguese thought it was theirs. No one thought to ask the Africans what they thought. Rhodes wanted to annex Africa first, then the rest of the world, and then start on the planets. Recolonizing America was on his to-do list. *Enough* was not in his vocabulary.

How does this differ from Mr. Hitler? you ask. It doesn't. Rhodes stole so much real estate that he became the "Rt. Hon." C. J. Rhodes. You could be "right honourable" too if you would steal as much as Rhodes did, for God and the Mother Country. Oxford even gave him an honorary doctorate.

Some say that Rhodes was a great man, but what is greatness? Do great men wear old tennis shoes and white flannel trousers?[140] Do great men lapse into falsetto giggles? At times he even squeaked! Are great men afraid of Princess Radziwill? Others say he was the devil's agent, but this is unlikely, as he had more money than the devil had. It is said that he ruined Africa. Well, if he hadn't, someone else would have—probably the Germans. Some say that Rhodes was racist, but he was willing to exploit people of any color. He believed in "one man, one vote" for South Africa. Guess who was the one man.

Fortunately, Rhodes did not get very far on his to-do list. He died young, without annexing even one planet, because he had tubercular lungs, a "dickie" heart, clogged arteries, and badly swollen ambitions. He ate too much

---

[140] At least he wore trousers!

and smoked too much and got his exercise by horseback riding, not realizing that it was his horse that was getting the exercise. When his doctor prescribed rest, Rhodes went shooting in Scotland. Shooting was his idea of resting. He died in 1902 and was buried in "Rhodesia." His last words were, "Turn me over, Jack."

But Rhodes accomplished much in his short life. Never mind that it should not have been accomplished at all. He killed tens of thousands of people, but it was for a good cause, he said. Even Philip Jourdan, his secretary and lap dog, admitted that Rhodes was "not a saint in the accepted meaning of the word." Without Rhodes there would have been no Boer War, just big gaps in the history books. You would notice that something was missing.

Leaving no wife or children to spend his money, he created the Rhodes scholarships to propagandize colonials (and even Americans) at Oxford. He forgot to exclude blacks from his scholarships, probably because he could not imagine one civilized enough to qualify for one. Heathen savages at Oxford? Indeed! Women were excluded, however, as manliness was a requirement. Rhodes himself would not have qualified for a Rhodes scholarship, as there were moral qualifications. Rhodes believed that his money could bring about the millenium, but it came anyway.

Some say that Rhodes will have a glorious second coming, but no sign of him yet. His influence in South Africa is fading away. The "Rhodesias" have been given more appropriate names. But the big hole at Kimberley is still there to remember him by.

VI

Popular Hate Figures

Kaiser Wilhelm II

Benito Mussolini

Adolf Hitler

Francisco Franco

Kaiser Wilhelm II

Kaiser Wilhelm II was overbearing as a child, even for a Hohenzollern. He liked to bite people on the legs and hit them with sticks. Everyone hoped he would grow out of it, but he had a lifelong talent for expressing himself, which was unfortunate.

His mother said his head was stuffed with rubbish. She wanted to padlock his mouth. His grandmother, Queen Victoria, said he needed a "good skelping."[141] He called her an "old hag." As a matter of fact, she *was* an old hag, but did he have to mention it? She wondered whether it was necessary for him to invite himself to England so often. It was, because who else would invite him? He was spying on the English navy.

---

[141] A thrashing administered by a Scottish person.

Wilhelm, or Willy, was born with a withered left arm, which he blamed on the "taint" of his English blood. Sometimes it seemed he had a withered left brain as well.[142] But he determined that his physical handicaps would not prevent him from becoming what he aspired to be: a reincarnation of Frederick the Great at his worst. Indeed, he could rattle sabers better with one arm than most people could with two.

Showing a precocious aptitude for mindless violence, he loved blood sports, such as murdering stags and stabbing boars repeatedly with a ceremonial sword called a *Saufeder*.[143] Willy loved the military, especially the badges and uniforms. It was said that if you offered him plum pudding he would change into the uniform of a British field marshal. Willy believed that war was life's greatest adventure, that Germany's past would have been a colossal bore without its glorious bloodbaths. He idolized the Huns and felt it unfair that he was not allowed to behead people the way Frederick the Great did back in the good old days of German greatness, before the "idiotic civilians" took over.

Willy saw himself as a romantic hero out of *Lohengrin* or Sir Walter Scott. He stood in a stance so aggressive that a full-length portrait of him was said to be a "declaration of war." But beneath the pompous ferocity was a timorous neurotic, a milksop afraid of his own grandmother! Willy had more in common with Walter Mitty than with Walter Scott. The "Supreme War Lord" didn't look so fearsome when the wax in his moustache melted. In fact, Willy was a wimp!

It was said that Willy was fond of practical jokes, but his jokes were not very practical. He liked to pinch and slap people on their behinds, but he really should not have done it to the king of Bulgaria! It started an

---

[142] But Lytton Strachey said he was "headstrong."
[143] Willy missed his calling. He would have been happier as a pig sticker in an abattoir, but it is too late for that now.

international incident. What was practical about that? He liked to pop spoons into the cleavages of ladies. Anything for a laugh! People did laugh at his pranks; they were afraid not to!

Aboard his yacht Willy insisted that everyone do calisthenics on deck before breakfast. Then he would topple over elderly gentlemen when they were in a vulnerable posture. Usually they missed the humor in this. There was no shortage of deck chairs on his yacht, but Willy still preferred to sit on Duke Charles Edward of Saxe-Coburg-Gotha.

The imperial dachshunds were as ill-behaved as their master. They liked to pee on the dresses of high-class ladies. Willy's household staff wanted to poison them discreetly, but were afraid he would replace them with Great Danes (Bismarck had Great Danes).

Willy expected his guests to earn their keep by entertaining him. They dressed in outlandish costumes to make him laugh. Count Görtz, always a favorite, could make animal noises. One of Willy's cabinet ministers made the supreme sacrifice for his kaiser and country. He collapsed and died while dancing for Willy in a ballerina's tutu. But aides were afraid to play tennis with Willy, for fear of driving a ball into the imperial stomach.

Although his taste in art made him the laughingstock of the art world, Willy was not without talent. He could imitate the sound of champagne being opened and poured into a glass. His other talents included handing out medals and portraits of himself.

Willy preferred to be called the "Most High" or the "All Highest." He liked to ride in parades with Bismarck and Hindenburg so he could pretend that the cheering was directed at his own august presence. His brother Henry made speeches lavish in praise of the "sublime, mighty, beloved kaiser"; they might have been more convincing if they had not been written by Willy himself. Some people even kissed Willy's hand! He saw no harm in it. He believed he was infallible, but was wrong about that. He complained that no one understood or appreciated him. He was right about that.

Willy approached issues with an open mouth instead of an open mind. There were demands that he be muzzled, but no volunteers. One citizen served two years in prison for calling him a "*windbeutel*" (windbag), even though it was true.

Willy would not allow anyone to insult his parents, as he reserved that right for himself. He did not like his mother, and put her under house arrest. She didn't like him either because he was not at all like her father, Prince Albert. It seems hardly fair to expect a baby to be like Prince Albert.[144] Willy's genes got mixed up somehow. Everyone was hoping he would inherit his father's good looks and his mother's brains. Instead he got stuck with his mother's looks and about half his father's brains.

Willy married Princess Augusta Victoria Frederica Louisa Feodora Jenny of Schleswig-Holstein-Sonderburg-Augustenburg. Naturally he didn't want to mess with all that, so he called her Dona. Queen Victoria called her "odious." Dona was so placid that she reminded everyone of a cow. After all, she was a Holstein. Dona and Willy were made for each other. She was cowlike and he was bullheaded. Dona has been called insignificant, but how could anyone be insignificant who could survive marriage to Kaiser Wilhelm?

Willy's married life was about what you might expect. But he was not home much, as he liked to gad about on his yacht, paying goodwill visits. Arriving unannounced and uninvited, with his enormous retinue, he would throw households into a panic.[145] Too much goodwill can be overwhelming. Willy usually went away in excellent humor, leaving a trail of sick headaches

---

[144] Like most babies, Willy looked more like Winston Churchill.
[145] Hosts were expected to feed and entertain them all, maybe even kiss Willy's hand.

behind him. Meanwhile Dona would be left at home with the children, chewing her cud and pouting because Willy would rather flirt with his friend Philip Eulenburg than with her. Willy liked to pat good-looking young officers on their bottoms.

Willy and Dona had lots of children; too many, in fact. Their eldest son was so awful that people didn't even want Willy to retire! But Willy was delighted that most of his children were sons, as he regarded girls as useless creatures, except for breeding and housework. He preferred the company of men. After all, how can you have a meaningful conversation with someone who has no appreciation of the finer points of a dreadnought?

Willy believed that God was German and foreigners were inferior. He liked French champagne but insisted that it be relabeled *Burgeff-Grün* so he could pretend it was German. He had a simple solution to the Serbian problem: wipe out the Serbs. Some of his best friends were Jewish but you should have heard what he said about them when they were not around! (He said they were no better than Jesuits.) "The Japanese are devils," he said, with characteristic indiscretion. Most of all, Willy worried about "the Yellow Peril." He felt the Oriental races were up to no good. Indeed, there were not many people Willy trusted. He tended toward paranoia.

He had mixed feelings about the English. He read their *Daily Graphic* and enjoyed their tea, but their naval superiority got on his nerves. So did his Uncle Bertie, King Edward VII. Willy was half English himself. In fact, if Willy's mother had been a man, Willy would have been king of England. Or would he? Willy wanted the English to take him seriously so he started building a navy to rival theirs. Naturally this scared them out of their wits.[146] Not to worry, Willy reassured them, his battleships were intended for "the Yellow Peril," although they couldn't carry enough coal to reach the Orient. A designer of ships, Willy invented one that could do all sorts of marvelous things. The only problem was that it wouldn't float.

Willy believed it the duty of a kaiser to leave Germany bigger than he found it; to leave behind some little Alsace or Lorraine to remember him by. Poland would be nice. But he insisted he had no territorial ambitions. Except maybe Malta, the Azores, Madeira, and the Cape Verde Islands. The Belgian Congo, the French Congo, Longwy-Briey, Courland, Lithuania, Luxembourg. Liege, the coast of Flanders, Morocco. Samoa and Georgia. He was not interested in Africa, as "niggers and palm trees" were not worth fighting over, but Germans

---

[146] And you wonder why World War I happened!

were entitled to a "place in the sun." This was before they discovered Torremolinos and Las Palmas.

Willy is often blamed for World War I but is that fair? After all, didn't he sit it out, like a wallflower? Nobody wanted him at the front, as both sides already had their hands full with the mud and the cooties. Believing he was too important to be near the fighting, he spent the war years at a safe distance, sipping tea, playing cards, sawing wood, and studying the language of the ancient Hittites. And rattling sabers, of course, but in private. He had not wanted a big war, only a little war followed by a big victory parade.

When the outlook turned bleak, he turned to God, praying and weeping. Then he would rant, "Take no prisoners!" and "Kill as many of the swine as you can!" President Wilson offered to discuss peace with any official German representative, except Willy. But Willy refused to abdicate, saying that descendants of Frederick the Great do not abdicate. So Prince Max abdicated him when he wasn't looking.

Fleeing to Holland with several crates of champagne, Willy became a nice old country gentleman retired from business. Here he spent many years harmlessly playing with his toy soldiers, sticking colored pins into maps, and denying that he was guilty of starting the Great War. He blamed the English. He collected Prussian Army badges, wrote a book about gorgons, read P. G. Wodehouse, and converted the trees in his neighborhood into neatly-stacked piles of firewood. His memoirs are worth reading, if you enjoy fiction. When Dona died he married another silly woman, Princess Hermione, who thought Hitler was going to restore Willy to power. But Hitler had other plans.

Many people wanted Willy hanged, but he died in bed, more peacefully than he deserved to, at a ripe old age. He said he wanted to be remembered as "William the Great, a Prince of Peace"[sic]. But most people prefer to remember him as "Kaiser Bill, the Mad Dog of Europe."

You ask, did Willy start the great war? Well, he didn't really mean to. It was sort of an accident.[147] He said he was only trying to keep up with the British! It is true that his saber rattling tended to drive the neighbors into entangling alliances, but remember, Willy was not great enough to start such a big war all by himself.

Pope Leo XIII said that Willy was the "spiritual heir of Charlemagne." Pope Leo put snuff up his nose.[148]

---

[147] He didn't know it was loaded!
[148] Sorry about the non sequitur.

Benito Mussolini

If you like schoolyard bullies, you'll love Benito Mussolini. He delighted in terrorizing the other children in Predappio, Italy. He loved to pull their hair and throw rocks at them, and ride little girls as if they were horses. He even took on bigger kids, and declared war on his third grade teacher! But he was not stupid. In elementary school he majored in human resources,[149] with related minors in assault and battery. That is, when he was not being expelled for punching up the other kids.

But no wonder he was mixed up! His father read Marx and Machiavelli to him and his mother took him to church! There were two icons on the wall in the Mussolini

---

[149] organizing gangs

home: Garibaldi and the Madonna of Pompeii. What was a poor kid to think?

Mama Mussolini thought her pugnacious little rogue would amount to something someday, but who could figure out what? Going to jail was a family tradition and, as soon as he was old enough, he dutifully carried it on— usually for dueling, known in the vernacular as "making spaghetti." Going to jail was known as "taking a rest." He took a rest.

When he reached draft age, Mussolini went tramping in Switzerland. Here he decided he was a Nietzschean superman, but there were no job openings for supermen so he lived on money from Mama, or panhandled or did odd jobs. They say he even slept under bridges. When he became interested in class struggle, the authorities became interested in him and expelled him from Switzerland.

After zigzagging for a while from one ism to another, he became a Socialist newspaper editor. There were two kinds of Socialists in those days:

* Reformist Socialists used legal means to get what they wanted, such as diplomacy, compromise, reason, the ballot box, strikes, "milk and water remedies," incremental improvements, invertebrate accommodation and shameless groveling, pussyfooting and mollycoddling, back scratching and bootlicking, cajoling and palavering, friendly persuasion, bloodless gradualism, parliamentary pea-shooting, charm, and being nice.

* Revolutionary Socialists used extralegal means, such as barricades, rioting, arson, bombs, cudgels, thuggery, assassination, castor oil, peeing on the walls of government buildings, boxing ears, truculence, brute force, nastiness, mayhem, and running over people with motorcycles.

Our man was the latter type and despised the former, calling them "spaghetti Socialists." He was no "toothless, clawless lion." He wanted no "bloodless reforms." He wanted to kick butt and bop heads because he was a superman bursting at the seams with industrial - strength testosterone! Mussolini believed that there were only two kinds of people in the world: those who oppressed others and those who were oppressed by others. He decided he would rather join the former. The sword was mightier than the pen, he insisted, because it was awkward to lop off heads with a pen.

Italy was old, gouty, and torpid, thought Mussolini. It ought to be a great power, as in the good old days of the Caesars, good for something besides spaghetti parlors, tour guiding, and opera singers. Greatness would require kicking some butt, of course, but no problem! He was willing. When World War I came, he saw it as opportunity knocking, a chance for Italy to unite, as the Germans had united under Bismarck, into a lean, mean, world machine. A chance for him to kick butt and play superman. But Socialists were weak-livered peacemongers, he thought, who wabbled and whined too much. They were paralyzed by ethical constraints[150] and offered insufficient opportunities for advancement to a superman in a hurry. So he broke with them in 1914.

Meanwhile, fascism flourished in the chaotic conditions after the war. Mussolini got in front of it, marched on Rome, and forced himself upon the king. Caught between Mussolini and civil war, the king opted for the former and that's how Mussolini became *Il Duce* in 1922. He had always wanted to be *Il Duce* of something. He pretended to be a strong, resolute, Nietzschean superman who could restore order and maybe even make the trains run on time. It worked; the Italian people fell for it. Or were they pushed?

The early fascists were a mixed bag of mixed-up students, military veterans out of a job, soreheads, goons,

---

[150] They thought that human life had value. You can't get ahead thinking like that, said Mussolini.

thugs, muckers, and social flotsam. Sure they were rowdies, but at least they were not Bolsheviks! They had a terrible weapon for purging leftists of their "wrong" thinking—castor oil. Yes, the same vile stuff your mother gave you, but they did Mom one better. They spiked it with diesel fuel for added emphasis, and applied it by the liter. There was no defense against such a weapon.

In 1918, fascism was a movement without a program. By 1921 it had become a party and a problem, with a militia of armed thugs and a supply of castor oil. In 1923 the Fascist Blackshirts joined the Nationalist Blueshirts and together they made Italy black and blue. In the thirties the Blackshirts joined the Nazi Brownshirts in helping the Falangist Blueshirts against the Reds in Spain. It was a colorful time.

The king was an obstacle to Italy's greatness, thought Mussolini. How could any nation become great under such an effete little idiot as Victor Emmanuel? But Victor controlled the military, so Mussolini had to humor him. He set up a diarchy with him, like a marriage with two bedrooms. Later the church moved in, like a mother-in-law, and made it a triarchy. Mussolini insisted that *Il Duce* always be capitalized, but the king was to be relegated to the lowercase, where he belonged. Mussolini had a pecking order to maintain. Even pronouns that referred to Him were to be uppercased!

Mussolini became a nationalist, believing that Italy was the only nation worth fretting about. His Fascist agenda featured:

* Imperialism—a natural expression of vitality, said Mussolini. Big fish eat little fish, and who wants to be a little fish?

* Militarism—Mussolini mobilized all Italy into a huge boot camp. The military ethic was applied to all, even to little old ladies and children. There was no room for weak-livered milksops because war was the natural state of human beings, the greatest

thing since macaroni met cheese. Peace was "menopausal" sissy stuff.

* Repression—Liberty was all right for cave men, said Mussolini, but Italians were incapable of making decisions, so the state had to make decisions for them.

* Racism/Elitism—Mussolini didn't mind Jews if they were reasonably white and card-carrying Fascists and didn't try to marry his daughter. The trouble was that if you scratched a Jew hard enough you'd often find a Bolshevik underneath, sometimes even a Mason or Zionist. Mussolini had no trouble hating blacks in Ethiopia, but had to practice to hate white people. Eventually he mastered the art and could hate almost anybody, at will.

* Corporatism—also known as bottom line or "delivering the goods." It meant that production was planned from on high, by Mussolini himself. It looked good on paper but Italy was as wretched as ever under Mussolini, even before he got it bombed to rubble.

In 1935 Mussolini decided to confront "the Ethiopian problem," which was that Ethiopia had not yet been grabbed. War was necessary, he said, because he wanted more Fascist babies and needed a place to put them. Ethiopia was good enough to be Italian, he thought, although its people were barbarous savages. He tried to civilize them with bombs, tanks, poison gas, machine guns, flame throwers, howitzers, and general nastiness, but it did not seem to work. Instead of civilizing the Ethiopians, it made the Italians barbarous savages. Mussolini was disappointed that too few Italians were killed in the war, which had been won at too low a price to reinvigorate the national character. But it was a good little war, and there would be bigger and better wars in the future, to prove the mettle of his Fascists. He would see to that! The war was "magnificent sport" and "exceptionally good fun," said Mussolini's son Vittorio, who enjoyed playing "hunt the Moor" with his airplane.[151]

Mussolini thought Hitler was giving dictators a bad name. He didn't like him, but didn't know what to do about him; who did? So he joined him.[152] Sure, peace would be nice, some day, but what was the hurry? There would be plenty of time for peace and justice later, after he had overrun a few more countries. Meanwhile, he wanted to be on the winning team and Hitler looked like a winner. Although in 1934 Mussolini had called Hitler a *pulcinella* (buffoon), in time he became lacky to that *pulcinella*. Winston Churchill called Mussolini "a tattered lacky" and a swine.

Wars were necessary, said Mussolini, to test the mettle of a people. Sure enough, his wars revealed some heavy mettle in his own people; too bad they died in the process of being tested and were of no further use to Italy or to themselves. Mussolini was delighted by the bombing of Naples in 1941, saying that it would "harden the breed." The breed did indeed harden, with rigor mortis.

Mussolini insisted that imperial expansion was necessary to accommodate Italy's surplus population, but then he taxed bachelors for not contributing to that surplus. Well, it made sense to him! He liked cannon fodder, insisting that each Italian family do its patriotic duty and produce as many Fascist babies as possible, at least twelve per family. Babies were fine, as long as they were Italian, because resolute, card-carrying, Fascist babies would be needed in his future wars for living space.

Mussolini met his wife Rachele when she was eight years old. He could tell that she was his type because she

---

[151] But Vittorio Mussolini complained that he got no "satisfaction" from bombing the miserable mud huts of Ethiopians. He felt he had been born to bomb better things.
[152] The British and the French were sore about Ethiopia, so Hitler was the only ally available.

liked to throw rocks at people and shoot starlings. Years later, in 1910, they had an accident together and named it Edda. This meant that they were almost married! They had four more children, but fell short of their quota of twelve. I don't know how many extramarital babies Mussolini contributed to the cause. He probably didn't know himself. Women were of little importance, he said. Just "a pleasant parenthesis" in the life of a man. He was against female suffrage, insisting that he did not need the votes of women—or any other votes, for that matter.

Mussolini has been called a pinhead because his vision of government was a hierarchy culminating in a pinhead. But he was not a conehead or zip.[153] His government was a mean machine, driven by pure will-to-power, without confusing traces of ideology or principle.

When Mussolini said, "Only one person in Italy is infallible," he was not referring to the pope. He had no use for the church or the popes, feeling that Fascism was the only religion he would ever need. He even tried to abolish Christmas, since it only reminded people of the birth of a peacemongering Jew who gave the world debilitating socialist theories and uppity popes. But alas, Santa Claus proved to be more popular than he was. Christmas stayed, by popular demand.

After 1930, the Fascist Party imposed a moral code on its members, if you can call it that. It was written by Mussolini himself, who said that conscience was "a pair of breeches that could be lowered whenever necessary." Pope Pius XI said that Mussolini was "a man sent to us by God." Then why didn't God give the man some breeches? Mussolini believed he was beyond good and evil. Indeed, he was beyond good. Mussolini liked to boast that he had eliminated the Mafia. And he did too, by welcoming it into his regime.

---

[153] He was a muttonhead.

"Never smile in public," Mussolini advised his Fascists, believing that smiling detracted from one's gravitas. Try to look fierce, but benevolent.

Mussolini was a workaholic, but kept fit by exercising power. He had many hobbies, including soccer, playing the violin, reckless driving, a pet lioness, pet mistresses, and redrawing maps. Art bored him, but he had a connoisseur's appreciation for captured enemy flags. He didn't care much about clothes or fashion, except for black shirts. He stopped wearing bowler hats when Laurel and Hardy started wearing them.

Mussolini wanted to start a dynasty, as the Caesars had, but by 1941 his popularity had taken a nosedive because of "the Mussolini hole" (the last hole in the belts of hungry Italians). His popularity was linked to the availability of food, especially eggs.[154] Socialism promised a chicken in every pot, but Fascism couldn't deliver even a bluddy[155] egg! He also caught hell for the Allied bombs that fell on Italy and was deposed in July 1943. Even his son-in-law voted against him! He became the most hated man in Italy. He had worried that peace might break out before he had enough dead Italians to sit at the peace conference as a belligerent, but he needn't have worried. He became a dead Italian himself in April 1945, before peace broke out.

Despite Mussolini's attempts to harden it, Italy remained the "soft underbelly" of the Axis bloc. He said he wanted to make Italy great, respected, and feared. Well, one out of three is not bad. He tried to keep up with the Nazis, but bet on the wrong horse. And no, the trains did not run on time!

Mussolini's life teaches us that testosterone poisoning should be treated in its early stages, before it starts a war.

---

[154] The coffee shortage was "real martyrdom," said Rachele Mussolini.
[155] Not a typo.

Adolf Hitler

In hindsight, Adolf Hitler looks pretty bad, but in 1937 Germans thought him no worse than your average lunatic. Didn't he provide jobs during the Depression? And Bolshevik-free washrooms? Didn't he make Germany bigger, if not better?[156] Didn't he thumb his nose at the Versailles Treaty and the West? Germans loved him for that! Even God was fooled for a while. God blessed Hitler's weapons, according to Hitler. But after a while there was talk about this angry man with the ugly smudge under his nose. Was he really such a good idea?

---

[156] In 1936, Hitler was more popular than Jesus because he took the Rhineland. What did Jesus ever take?

Not if you were Jewish. Hitler thought Jews were subhuman swine and not real Germans. They stabbed fatherlands in the back when you weren't watching. They started world wars, all by themselves. They danced around golden calves. They were Bolsheviks and capitalists at the same time. They were repulsive and bow-legged, but irresistible to Aryan women. So Hitler decided to tidy up the landscape by sending the Jews elsewhere, but where? Everybody seemed to have enough Jews already, so he tried the "final solution." The trouble with the final solution was that Hitler was the problem. He claimed he was only speeding up evolution, but there was nothing natural about his selection. Some say that Hitler's grandfather was a Jew. I can't say for sure—never met the man—does it matter? Germans were never quite sure what a Jew was, whether half Jews were still Jews, or three-eighths Jews who had German war medals. And what about three-sixteenths Jews who were married to Aryans and hated Bolsheviks but spoke Yiddish and ate gefilte fish and cheese blintzes? It got complicated! But Hitler thought he knew Jews when he saw them, by their indefinable quality of swinishness. To clarify matters, after 1938 all Jews had to be named either Israel or Sarah, by law. No Wagnerian names were allowed them.

Jews were infected with racial tuberculosis, said Hitler, which however did not show up on chest X-rays. It was in the blood, he insisted, but did not show up on blood tests. Jews were a plague, although only one percent of the population. Aryans were a race, said Hitler, but Jews were a fungoid growth, an abscess contaminated with democracy, Bolshevism, and God knows what else. Most historians today regard Jews as just folks, but Hitler believed they were leeches. On 26 July 1942 Hitler's doctor applied leeches to Hitler, but they refused to suck. Can you blame them?

There were three kinds of people in Hitler's Germany: desirables, undesirables, and useful undesirables, known as honorary Aryans. These last were rare. Hitler's bankers warned him that persecuting Jews was bad for business. Otherwise, no one seemed to mind, except Jews.

Jews were not the only swine, according to Hitler, who did not like homosexuals either, or gypsies or defective people or Social Democrats or Slavs or Jesuits. In fact, Hitler didn't much care for anybody who did not have blonde hair, blue eyes, fair skin, pink cheeks, a narrow nose, even narrower political views, and blood purer than an Aryan baby's butt. Hitler admitted in 1943 that he had only two friends in the world: Fräulein Braun and Blondi, his Alsatian bitch.

Hitler had lots of *fräuleins*. He liked his women sweet and stupid, and most of them were. They seemed to have one thing in common: suicide attempts. Some succeeded—it was not easy being *der führer's* significant other! Hitler was impotent, said Lord Bullock.[157] Maybe so, but he could erect his right arm any time he pleased. Fräulein Braun[158] made the supreme sacrifice for Hitler: she gave up smoking. She was mostly for decoration, but Hitler finally married her in 1945 to make her respectable. It didn't work. You can't get respectable by marrying someone like Hitler.

Hitler had lots of dog friends. In fact, most of his friends were dogs. He preferred Alsatians of pure Aryan descent. Fräulein Braun preferred Basset hounds. The less said about their descents the better. On 6 February 1935, Fräulein Braun complained to her diary, "If only I had a puppy, then I wouldn't be so lonely." Alas, Hitler was not in touch with his inner puppy.

Hitler's father was a brute who did not believe in sparing the rod. With a son like Hitler, can you blame him? He thrashed Hitler daily, whether he needed it or not. But Hitler was grateful to his father for one thing he did back in 1876: he changed his name from Schicklgru-

---

[157] How did *he* know?
[158] Known as "the stupid cow."

ber to Hitler. Without that change, the *Heil Hitler* mantra that stirred the *führer* cult to mass hysteria would not have been the same. Hitler's mother was nice, she doted on him, but after she died there was no one left to dote on poor Hitler except his dog Foxl.[159] Someone stole Foxl in 1917 and Hitler never got over it. "The swine who stole my dog doesn't realize what he did to me," he protested. Was it a Jew who stole Hitler's dog? Did he think the damned dog was worth changing world history?[160]

Even aside from his dogs, Hitler's family tree was a mess. His mother might have been a granddaughter of her husband's father. Got that? She called her husband "Uncle Alois." And Hitler did things with his niece that would have embarassed Krafft-Ebing.[161] Hitler liked to be kicked and peed on, according to those who should know. In time there was no shortage of volunteers.

As a youth, Hitler sank to the bottom of society. No one believed he would ever amount to anything. World War I was his first real job and it was more fun than shooting rats with his airgun, so he refused to accept that it was over or that Germany had lost. He wanted to make it the best of three. He believed that willpower could conquer all, as it did in Wagnerian operas, so he could not wait to start act two of the Great War.

Germans were in a nasty mood in 1923 because a kilo of butter cost 168 million marks. The liberal Weimar government caught hell for it, so Hitler tried to seize power in a harebrained scheme called the Beer Hall Putsch. It didn't work out and Hitler was sent to prison, where he wrote *Mein Kampf,* his blueprint for world mayhem. Hardly anyone took it seriously, but Hitler also had a talent for inflammatory oratory, a special gift for appealing to the gutter emotions of audiences. Torrents of

---

[159] Some sources say Füchsl. Honestly, does it matter?
[160] Hitler and Foxl had much in common. They both liked to hunt rats.
[161] His niece called him "Uncle Wolf," and why not?

cosmic blather oozed from his drooling mouth, as he ranted and raved to the point of near orgasm. His hoarse, sweating, paroxysms of rage made for a good show, and Germans flocked to hear his world-class tantrums. His speeches should rightly be called screeches, said Herbert Shelton. Soon Hitler had a devoted following and was calling himself *führer*. He had been calling for a superman to save Germany but no volunteers came forward, so he decided, what the hell, why not me? Will I do? God wanted *him* to rid Germany of Jewish "vermin!" That's why assassination plots against him always failed— divine protection. Or was it the luck of the devil?

Hitler thought parliamentary government was for sissies and elections were nonsense, but he was on probation and not a German citizen, so he had to behave himself, for a while. Nazis would have to hold their noses and outvote the liberal sissies instead of shooting them. What the Nazis needed now was a crisis, and the stock market graciously obliged on Black Friday, 1929.

The Great Depression made everybody greatly depressed, and there was no Prozac in those days. The Weimar government caught the blame, as usual, and people wanted change, so Hitler offered himself as the candidate for change. That he was indeed! Germans wanted a firm hand at the helm, so Hitler offered them his iron fist. He offered them passion, destiny, heroic struggle, a national rebirth of the fatherland, cheap butter. It sounded good. The liberals offered only the usual boring, namby-pamby, bourgeois bookkeeping. Their insipid pacifistic bilge could not fire men's spirits, said Hitler. At least he was not a Bolshevik, so President Hindenburg, in a fit of senility,[162] appointed him chancellor in 1933.

As chancellor, Hitler wasted no time in outlawing Jews, Social Democrats, and practically everybody else.

---

[162] and politics. Hindenburg was involved in a nasty scandal that Hitler agreed to cover up.

He grabbed newspapers, labor unions, Jewish businesses, the Rhineland, then started grabbing countries, with very little trouble until in 1939 he went into Poland. The trouble with Poland was that the Poles shot back. Also, there were lots of Jews in Poland to be disposed of. But where? Let there be ghettos, said Hitler, and work camps. He had wanted an alliance with Britain, so that its mighty navy would protect his rear while he helped himself to Poland and Russia. But the Brits had better things to do than protect Hitler's rear, so he made a dinner date with Stalin and together they gobbled up Poland. No wonder Hitler had chronic indigestion!

This was fun, Hitler decided, as he gobbled up more countries. He was having the time of his life, and Mussolini and Matsuoka hopped aboard for the joyride. Hitler claimed he had never signed the Versailles Treaty so he was not bound by it. His hobby was collecting— countries, that is. And why not? It was so easy. Soon he had almost a complete Baltic set and the war had assumed Wagnerian proportions; but no problem, Hitler had always wanted to be a Wagnerian hero. Besides, Germany also was assuming Wagnerian proportions.

By 1941, Hitler's popularity was holding, despite the high price of sausage rolls, but low mutterings of discontent were being heard, because this time he could not blame the butter shortage on Weimar liberals. Hitler liked guns more than butter because it was hard to kill Jews with butter—it took too long. But most Germans still preferred butter.

Hitler believed in positive thinking, so he saw no reason not to invade Russia in 1941. Wasn't it ripe for collapse because of its inner Jewish rot? Didn't it have lots of oil that Joe Stalin could not be trusted with? Wasn't it like the Wild West and hadn't he always wanted to be a cowboy? Didn't it have lots of living space to expand into, once the Jews and Slavs had been cleared out? So he invaded, but instead "General Winter" and "General Mud" cleared Hitler out. His troops had to retreat like Napoleon's, with their frozen tails between their frozen legs. Be warned: positive thinking can be very dangerous.

By 1943 it was obvious to everyone—except Hitler—that his war was lost. He declared "total war" so that it could be totally lost. Two more fronts opened up and the Germans were in a fix even Wagner could not have wiggled out of. Germany was a mess from Allied bombing, and its own allies were deserting ship, one by one. Romania took its oil wells when it left, and soon the Luftwaffe was running on empty. Hitler stopped making speeches, and even screeches. What was there to say? The writing was on the wall. But he kept a positive attitude through it all, surrounding himself with optimists and yes-men, thus converting mere defeat into utter ruination. He was a runaway locomotive; his will-to-power had become will-to-catastrophe.

Finally, in 1945, Hitler euthanized himself and the Nazi bubble popped like a balloon. This is known as the final solution to the Hitler problem. Historians debate endlessly whether Hitler was the chicken or the egg. Did he surf a wave of nationalism or did he create it? In any case, the Nazi bubble popped when he did. Or did it relocate to Argentina?

Hitler was not very consistent. He believed in exterminating defective people but never seemed to notice Josef Goebbels' club foot, Rudolf Hess's buck teeth, or the paunchy, sparrow-brained, sausage-necked thugs in his SS. Not all Nazis were perfect, and their wives looked like washerwomen.[163] Hitler exterminated lots of mentally ill people without realizing that he was not quite all there himself. Hitler had "no phobias or obsessions," said his doctor, who was a case history himself.[164] But either Hitler had a messianic complex or he really was on a

---

[163] My apologies to washerwomen.
[164] Hitler's health improved whenever his doctor was incapacitated. It figures.

mission from God. You decide. Hitler has been called a hypochondriac, but in fact he really was a mess. He took so many pills is it any wonder he was more flatulent than a constipated Cape buffalo? But Hitler's flatulence was beyond the scope of this book.

Hitler has been likened to the Pied Piper of Hamelin but reminds me more of Captain Ahab in pursuit of a Jewish whale. He fancied himself as Siegfried awakening the sleeping fatherland with a kiss. Some say that Hitler was a great man. True, he may have been the greatest art thief of all time and the greatest hate figure of the twentieth century, but his grandiose plans to beautify Germany got it reduced to rubble—not a sign of greatness. Hitler killed millions of people, but they were mostly the wrong people and it didn't do a bit of good. His Thousand Year Reich fell short by 988 years. Still, for a high-school dropout, twelve years was something.

I hear you complaining: why don't I ever say anything positive about poor Hitler? Yes, I know, Mr. Hitler is dead and it is not cool to badmouth the dead. Well, OK then, if you insist. Mr. Hitler liked canaries. He liked pudding and cream puffs and asparagus tips. He liked Shirley Temple movies.[165] He liked *Snow White and the Seven Dwarfs*. There now, that will have to do. This Pollyanna stuff goes against my grain. Besides, I already said that he euthanized himself. Wasn't *that* something positive?

Hitler had the charisma of a cockroach. His personality was mostly poisonality. Why then did the German people accept him so readily? They thought he was a winner. He offered them jobs, autobahns, Volkswagens, cheap butter, a compelling vision of a hegemonic future, a chance to merge their miserable wormlike existences into a great dragon. But mainly because he was not a Bolshevik.

---

[165] and King Kong movies.

Hitler's life teaches us never to steal a dog from a person of dubious mental stability. No dog is worth a world war. And beware the power of positive thinking. Look what it got him!

Francisco Franco

Francisco Franco loved law and order. That's why he joined the revolt against the lawful government of Spain and reduced the country to debris and ashes. Hundreds of thousands of people died in that revolt, but they might have been disorderly if he hadn't killed them. They might have done something unlawful.

As a child, little Paquito Franco thought of himself as a military machine. Spaniards later came to regard him as an institution. Historians disagree on whether he was human—there are arguments on both sides. In school he majored in horsemanship, shooting, and fencing—mostly shooting, which was a reflex reaction to him, as natural as breathing. He was like a gun dog, said his in-laws; as soon as he heard a shot he was off, to join the fun. He believed there were only two options in life: shooting and vegetating. A skinny kid with a "piping" voice,[166] he was forever being knocked about by the other boys. But he got the last laugh in 1936 by allowing a childhood chum to be executed.

After his "short and simple" childhood, Franquito went to military school, then to Morocco to play "hunt the Moor." Creating a foreign legion out of recycled criminals, deadbeats, goons, and desperadoes, he enjoyed beheading people and otherwise maintaining order. He learned how to divide and conquer—and sever—for fun and profit.

Rapidly rising in the ranks, Major Franquito married Carmen Polo in 1923, whose ambitions, equal to his own, were to reach epic, if not epidemic, proportions. In 1928 he became director of a military academy at Zaragoza. He did not allow textbooks at his school, believing in learning to shoot by shooting. Who needed a textbook to tell him what a trigger was for? His code of conduct for cadets was strict, however, as he did not allow grumbling. Liberals in the Second Republic closed his school in 1931, believing there was already enough shooting going on. Franco never forgave them for this. Shooting was his reason for living.

Franco shot and tortured thousands of people, but was always moral about it, as he never womanized, drank to excess, or smoked. He carried a relic of the hand of St. Teresa of Avila,[167] and believed he was on a mission for God. Franco was fearless in battle because he was blessed with *baraka*—divine protection. He felt that God had a vested interest in his safety, but don't believe the rumor that he was third cousin to the Virgin Mary. That one is a bit exaggerated. Yes, I know, Salvador Dali did say that

---

[166] Some sources say "fluted" voice. Probably somewhere between a flute and a bagpipe.

[167] He stole it from a general who had stolen it from a convent.

Franco was a saint, but didn't he also say that the train depot at Perpignan was the center of the universe? Franco wrote propaganda under various pen names. If you should come across a Senor Jakim Boor, for example, that would be our man. *Time* magazine called him "fat-bottomed Franco," but we won't go into that here. Others prefer to remember him as Paco, Generalisimo Fascisto Bastardo, or simply, "that pompous ass."

In 1936, liberals won the Spanish elections fair and square and tried to make liberal reforms, such as giving land to starving peasants. But some of the wilder leftists[168] were not satisfied with such palliatives; they wanted nothing short of revolution. They wanted a new millenium, with trumpets blaring and churches burning. The result was a right-wing backlash, known to history as the Spanish Civil War—actually a rebellion or religious crusade. It was necessary, said Franco, because the liberal government was a Trojan horse full of godless Bolsheviks and satanic Freemasons who were plotting to take over Spain. Red rats were gnawing into Spanish bank vaults. Foreign thoughts and ideas were infecting Spain. Bolsheviks were infecting Spanish washrooms. The leftist government could not maintain order, complained agents of disorder on the right, so it had to be replaced by the firm hand of a Fascist. Franco soon found his firm hand—actually his fist—in charge of the revolt. His pals Hitler and Mussolini joined him, but his greatest ally was the non-intervention of the West, which did not want to get involved, as who would?

The purpose of the revolt was to purge Spain of "undesirables"—pinkos, anarchists, Jews, Freemasons, Commie rats, "slave stock," and assorted riffraff—those that the Spanish Inquisition had missed. Franco did not want a quick victory; he wanted a gradual and thorough purge *(limpieza)* of undesirables. He wanted to give Spain a bath. What would be the point of victory if undesirables

---

[168] Some were so far left they were right.

would be still around stinking up the place? Franco wanted a unified Spain, but first the people had to be eliminated that he did not want to be unified with. He wanted to be father to the Spanish people—well, of about half of them, and there was plenty of room in hell for the other half. The cause of the war was sewers, said Count de Aguilera, because if it had not been for sewers the undesirable classes already would have perished from various salutary diseases.

Franco said he was willing to shoot half of Spain, if necessary, and I believe him because he tried to. He was willing to destroy Madrid to save it from Reds. But he *won* the war, so to speak, and it was worth it, he said in 1939, the skin on his nose intact. The Spanish *Patria* was "in a wild, anarchic state of disorder," said the Nazi high command, but it had had a good bath—a bloodbath—and would soon be acceptable in proper society, after a few thousand more undesirables had been launched into hell. Mussolini and Hitler were appalled by Franco's mass executions. After all, those leftist undesirables would have been useful as slaves. What a waste of man-hours! There were only ten thousand Freemasons in Spain but, with his remarkable olfactory powers, Franco was able to sniff out eighty thousand of them to purge in 1940.

The long civil war got to be a drag after a while so when World War II broke out Franco was not in the mood. He had fallen behind in his hunting and fishing, and had laurels to sit on. So he doubletalked Hitler with great effect, keeping him at bay with promises to join him any day now—after England collapses, when the armistice negotiations are getting under way. Meanwhile, he appeased Hitler with wolfram, submarine bases, and other perks. Franco came to be known as a man of peace because he kept out of the World War and kept Hitler away from Gibraltar. When Hitler made a pact with the Red rats in Russia, Franco thought it odd to be on the same team with them, but Hitler soon invaded them and things returned to normal.

The early years of Francoism were known as the *anos de hambre* because so many Spanish people starved to death. Franco's response to the food crisis was to write a novel, build a huge monument to the Nationalist war dead, recommend *austeridad* to the undesirable classes, and ship food to Nazi Germany in exchange for arms. None of these measures helped much. His "agrarian reforms" did not help either, because no matter how fast peasants died, they still outnumbered the food supply. Let them eat dolphin sandwiches, said Franco, and fish bread, and whatever they can find in rubbish bins. They were not real Spaniards after all, just undesirables. Feeding them would be counterproductive. Franco believed that bootblacks were Communist scum who should be shot. However, he had to spare them because his black-booted fascist thugs needed them to keep their boots shiny.

When by 1944 it became clear that Hitler and Mussolini were losers, their photos vanished from Franco's writing table and he started pitching woo to the West, which found him repugnant but decided to leave him alone, for fear of setting him off again. Let elections be announced, said Franco, to appease the West, but delayed—indefinitely. Some day, just you wait and see. Western plutocrats did find his anti-Communist paranoia endearing, but not enough to plug him into the Marshall Plan or NATO.

The fifties continued in the same dismal pattern, with galloping inflation, a crumbling economy, labor unrest. Franco was too preoccupied with slaughtering nature and sitting on his laurels to do much about these problems, which were too complicated to be solved by shooting. So he had to yield to technocrats, who had some autonomy because Franco hadn't a clue what they were up to. After twenty years of Franco, Spain was so poor that it had to accept help from liberals and Freemasons. "I seem to be turning communist," said Franco to his ministers, but hey, whatever worked! Politics had to yield to economics. He hooked up the Spanish cart to the international train, and hoped that his technocrats could create enough prosperity to keep a lid on dissent.

Although President Truman despised Franco, Ike felt an affinity with him because they shared the same passion for shooting birds, [169] so Franco charmed his way into the American camp. Americans were terrified of Red rats and Franco was a proven rat catcher. He gave the Yanks military bases in Spain; they gave him money and arms, while holding their noses and looking the other way.

We are a monarchy, said Franco, to appease the monarchists. Then where was the monarch? Never you mind, said Franco, some day we will have a monarch, just you wait and see. In the meantime, monarchy will have to wait because God has entrusted Spain to Franco, and you really shouldn't argue with God. "I don't resign," he said. "For me, it's straight from here to the cemetery." Having no intention of becoming a "queen mother," he would leave office "feet first." But Spain was still a monarchy, he insisted, while having monarchists arrested and imprisoned for conspiracy to restore the monarchy.

Franco did not like political parties. He allowed only one, and he was it. The people cannot be trusted with freedom, said Franco. Give them freedom and you get strikes, adolescent dustups, and Bolsheviks at the gates. Franco claimed to rule by "implied plebiscite," a safe claim since there was no way to know for sure.[170] There was an occasional mock election or referendum in Spain, but everybody knew that it was a mortal sin to vote against Franco and for the destruction of Spain by Red hordes from Moscow. Spaniards were guaranteed freedom, insisted Franco, but it would be freedom as defined by Franco. Spain had a "bill of rights" of sorts, but it wasn't much to brag about, and when it was suspended

---

[169] Franco liked fish and birds, if they were dead.
[170] But his victims were not implied.

in 1956, nobody noticed any difference. It was mostly a list of the civil rights that Franco was violating.

Franco was a workaholic. General Millan Astray said, "Our *caudillo* spends fourteen hours at his desk and doesn't even get up to piss." But Franco made time for hobbies, such as shooting, keeping important people waiting, shooting goats with machine guns,[171] surly disdain, more shooting, betting on football games, shooting cute little partridges, slaughtering whales and fish, golf, regal ostentation, spending the national patrimony, more shooting, etc. He also liked to paint; Preston says that Franco's art was "of more interest to the psychiatrist than to the art critic." Even apart from his oversized bladder, Franco considered himself a breed apart from ordinary mortals. His father agreed, calling him a "swine."[172]

During the sixties, Spanish liberals thought it was high time for the regime to open up and let in some fresh air. Franco disagreed, dismissing their protests as "adolescent dustups" inspired by the usual Reds and Freemasons. But Franco was not himself any more. He had adopted a new hobby—dozing off. His passionate tirades against Freemasons were supplanted by boring, droning, economic jargon and statistics, as if to suggest that things were going according to his plans. Marginalized by technocrats, he became an anachronism, increasingly cut off from reality, and people wondered about "the biological fact"—after Franco, what then?

What then indeed! The seventies brought the invasion of the yuppies, Nordic playboys, bikini-clad sun worshippers, short shorts and miniskirts. Torremolinos ran wild and became an international playground. Franco's own grandchildren became wild, emancipated

---

[171] Franco enjoyed slaughtering nature because he always won.

[172] But have you ever noticed Franco's uncanny resemblance to a roof rat? At times he looked gnomish.

yuppies. Ferdinand and Isabella turned over in their graves. By this time, Franco had lost control. His last years were engulfed in siestas and his regime crumbled as he did, but he refused to give up power until God relieved him of his duties. He had to protect his victory, after all. When God finally intervened on 20 November 1975, spontaneous dancing broke out in the streets of Basque towns. Champagne corks popped all over Spain. Democracy broke out and ran amok, the *movimiento* disbanded. By 1977, *Franquismo* was in ruins. Franco's estate at Valdefuentes was sold and used to make porno films.

Basically a rat catcher, Franco wanted everything "well and truly battened down," but after he was himself well and truly battened down, Red rats surfaced again in Spain and devoured ten percent of the vote in 1977.

Crozier argues that Franco could not have been a Fascist because Falangists, who were Fascists, were usually upset with him. No doubt Franco had a lot in common with Falangists, but they were soft on starving peasants. Real Fascists don't care about starving peasants, he thought. He was so a Fascist, said the United Nations in 1945. You'll have to decide for yourself. Franco denied being a Fascist, arguing in 1945 that he had only 26,000 political prisoners locked up. But what did he do with the 270,000 he had five years earlier? As we go to press, they are still missing and unaccounted for.[173]

Franco was not all bad. He drove Hitler nuts. Let's give him some credit for that! He saw himself as an instrument of destiny, an incarnation of the Spanish national soul, a modern day El Cid protecting the *Patria* from Commies, Freemasons, and Jews—as well as from pigeons and partridges. He was the messiah who saved

---

[173] Franco did not have all his prisoners shot; he had some strangled.

Spain from Bolshevism and Nazism. The problem was that he didn't save it from Francoism.[174]

His life teaches us that shooting people can indeed take you far, but you shouldn't expect it to solve all your problems.

---

[174] The Three Pillars of Francoism were the army, the church, and the Falange. They were known as "the family." The monarchy was a kind of unwanted Uncle Louie.

VII

Weirdos and Worse

Gilles de Rais

Casanova

Hetty Green

Rasputin

Gilles de Rais

Gilles de Rais was the world's wickedest man, and he wasn't even trying! One could argue that he has been surpassed in our own time, but for the fifteenth century he set the pace in depravity. Not having access to modern weapons of mass destruction, he had to kill people one at a time, which can get tedious. His methods were crude, but so was he.

Highborn in the Loire valley of France, he lusted after real estate during the Hundred Year's War, which was about real estate. In fact, he lusted after practically everything, except his wife. He thought it would be great fun to convert endless dross into endless gold, but how? The alchemy books failed him, so he sought out demons for their supernatural powers.

The trouble with demons was that they were not always honest, and drove hard bargains. They did not abide pettifoggers who offered them small bloodlettings for large favors. They were never satisfied with dead pigeons—not for anything big—so Gilles had to up the ante. He wanted to be fair about it. What would you have done? Supply was not a problem. There were plenty of ragged, hungry children eager to work as "pages" for the wealthy count. And there were always job openings because Gilles' pages had a way of mysteriously disappearing after a day or two, never to be seen again. But in fact it was not mere greed that drove Gilles. A connoisseur of sadistic bloodletting, he was already doing nasties to children for his own reasons. It turned him on, you know. He liked pain, as long as it was not his own.

If you are wondering what exactly he did that was so wicked, I can't give you all the lurid details, as this is a family essay. Community standards, you know. Besides, it might turn your brain to cottage cheese. His misdeeds were too naughty to talk about, even in French, so you'll have to take my word for it, he was horrid, and returned to his sins like a dog returns to its vomit. The charges against him included various abominations—use your imagination.

Well OK, unnatural debaucheries,[175] necrophilias, heresies, sorcery, wallowing in wickedness, wallowing in the elastic warmth of fresh human intestines, threatening a cleric, seeking out demons, ripping out hearts that were still in use, general swinishness, hacking away at the limits of the permissible, hacking away at the limbs of children, converting children into powder, you get the idea. I haven't got time to list them all. He was sort of like Montezuma the Aztec, except that he did not eat his victims. Or did he? Anyway, his motives were not the same as Montezuma's. He did not kill for food or to appease the harvest gods or to make the sun rise. He killed for some deep, dark, inner reasons that we'd better not go into.

---

[175] Even worse than natural debaucheries.

Gilles was not insane, not a mere case history out of Krafft-Ebing. He knew the difference between right and wrong but tilted toward wrong, at least in his Mr. Hyde phase. He had daily commerce with God, Jesus, the Virgin, and the saints in his Dr. Jekyll phase. That was why demons avoided him: he was too pious for their tastes. I'd have to say he was mixed-up. Gilles was the first sinner ever to go to hell with a piece of the true cross embedded in his arm.

So he never did get to meet a real demon, and had to communicate with them through evokers. The trouble with evokers was that you never knew what they might evoke—nor did they.[176] One of them evoked a demon in the form of a leopard that chased him away. (Probably Beelzebub; that was one of his tricks.) Others evoked demons who beat them up, or huge, green, winged serpents as big as dogs. It was scary business, evoking demons,[177] and it was not easy to get one, as they kept busy schedules and were not always punctual. Gilles never did get the hang of it. He burned magic powders, chanted all the right incantations, and always left the window open, but never did get to meet a real demon.[178] They didn't seem to trust him. They thought he was a piker, and a pious one at that.

Nor did women trust him. Despite his wealth, title, real estate, and sinister good looks, few women mistook Gilles for Mr. Right because his dark side was about as dark as sides get, dark enough to darken a whole attic, even a whole dungeon. His wife, Catherine de Thouars, never forgave him for the crude way he abducted her; she would have preferred to be abducted by a decent man. But Gilles was not the romantic type; he wanted her for her real estate. She was well-endowed—with real estate—

---

[176] Evokers were not licensed or accredited.

[177] Don't try this at home.

[178] After he died, he got to meet lots of demons. In fact, they are now his next-door neighbors.

and he found her big dowry very seductive.[179] It was not much of a marriage—her fantasies did not include him—but she gave him a daughter. Other than that, you needn't keep track of her.

Joan of Arc tells the dauphin she is from God.

In 1425, Gilles was introduced at the court of the French dauphin Charles. Some say that's where he picked up his bad habits, but he'd had a head start. The main item of court business in those days was driving the Goddens[180] and Burgundians out of France. The Goddens were winning until one day at Chinon when who should show up to offer her services but Joan of Arc! She said she

---

[179] Nye says she had a moon-shaped face, but doesn't say which phase of the moon.
[180] The English were known as Goddens or Goddamns.

was from God, so the dauphin figured, what the heck, she was worth a try. He needed God on his side because the Goddens had St. George on theirs. Gilles was assigned to protect Joan, in and out of battle, so they were together a lot, Beauty and the Beast.

You are probably wondering, did Gilles ever get fresh with Joan in camp after dark?[181] Not that it's any business of yours, but I think not. She had no real estate with which to attract him, so camp life was probably a bit on the dull side. Usually attired in male clothing and metallic body armor, she had a sword and knew how to use it.[182] She took orders from her heavenly voices,[183] and neither St. Catherine nor St. Margaret approved of Gilles. Nor did Joan's personal bodyguard, Jean d'Aulon.

Anyway, in 1429 Gilles and Joan helped relieve the siege of Orleans and made it into the history books. Both became superstars, but in very different categories. We don't know what he was up to on that fateful day in 1431 when she was roasted at Rouen, except that he was not protecting her. He didn't even offer to pay her ransom. Some say that her murder unhinged his mind, loosing his id upon the world, but his mind was not securely hinged in the first place. And his id had been out and about for some time.

By 1433 Gilles had fallen out of favor with the court. His services were no longer required—Joan no longer needed him—but he wasn't finished yet. Bloodletting had become a habit with him. Could he help it that it turned him on? You know how habits are; he needed a twelve-step program. Meanwhile, his id was running amok, under cover of religious ostentation.

---

[181] A heavenly light emanated from Joan. It kept Gilles awake nights.
[182] Her sword had supernatural powers, until she broke it on the sturdy rump of a female camp follower.
[183] Joan trusted her heavenly voices because they spoke good French, without a trace of an English accent.

In 1439 the plot thickened again. One of Gilles' procurers met a Gothic villain in Italy who claimed to be on familiar terms with a demon named Barron and could deliver messages to him. He could even get Barron to answer back—the real test of an evoker.[184] So naturally he brought him to France to meet Gilles. They did their thing in Gilles' attics, making sacrificial offerings to Satan, Belial, Beelzebub, Barron, and any other demons who might have been lurking in the neighborhood.

But Barron did not co-operate, and their alchemical experiments always failed. So no gold. Just huge piles of used dross and used bones. Gilles was very good at converting gold into dross but never succeeded in reversing the process. So he had to sell real estate. He preferred to sell it, then seize it back and sell it again. It was more cost-effective that way. Besides, sometimes he *had* to take back property in order to remove telltale corpses. He had been careless about his housekeeping.

Eventually there was talk. He should have known there would be talk. People started to connect the dots, and he'd left so many dots carelessly strewn about. When Gilles was in the neighborhood vital statistics tended to change rather noticeably.

He was brought to trial in 1440, charged with threatening a cleric. Gilles repented and expected God to forgive him and welcome him into heaven like his sidekick Joan of Arc, but to date no one has seen him there. Would it do to have Gilles in heaven, where his victims are serving as pages? That would be awkward, and I see no reason why serial killers need a patron saint. He thought there might be a suburb in heaven set aside for child killers who had repented, but his repentence was not convincing enough. He went to the other place.

I wish I could say that he meant well, but I see little evidence of that. There is no well-meaning way to reduce

---

[184] Any fool can talk to demons. The real test is getting them to answer back. And not running away when you get one.

children to powder. It usually doesn't happen by accident. Face it, he was a dirty, lowdown rat! Worse than Mr. Hyde in his cups! No doubt he was pious. His favorite saints were Michael and James, as Joan was not a saint until the twentieth century. She was considered a lunatic in her own time. He didn't have any favorite demons, as he never got to meet any. In fact, he was secretly afraid of demons, even more than they were of him. It seems hardly fair to call him a Satanist, as he never even met the guy! But he tried.

During his trial Gilles was excommunicated, which upset him so much that it was lifted, to his great relief. Then they killed him. After his execution, the citizens of Nantes whipped their sons—"to the blood"—every year on the anniversary of his death, just to keep them on the right track. It didn't help much, so in time they dropped the custom.

Gilles has defenders who point out that he confessed only under threat of torture, which is true. But then who put all those dead bones in his towers? Sure there were people who coveted his property, but you can't make a case out of that. He coveted their property too. What good is property if no one covets it? But serial killers are often misunderstood. It goes with the territory.

We don't know how many children he launched into eternity; he lost count after the first few dozen. The court mentioned 140 victims, but there were others. He had intended to reform his ways and make a penitential pilgrimage to the Holy Land, but serial killing is a full-time job. How could he work repentence into his busy schedule? There are only so many hours in the day.

They say that nobody is all bad, but he came pretty darn close. Still, he must have done something decent at some point in his life. What's that? You want to know what it was? Well ... let's see ... um ... er ... I'll get back to you later about that!

Why did he do it? For the carnal delight. That's what he said. You figure it out. He was a Scorpio, you know. Or was it the devilled meats he ate? He said he slipped into an abyss. It could happen to anyone in the Dark Ages, before street lighting.

Known as "The Beast of Extermination" or "Bluebeard" or "The Fiend from Hell," Gilles is not to be confused with the fictional Bluebeard, who murdered his fictional wives. Gilles had only one wife and felt that she was not worth murdering. Besides, she kept out of his way. Their daughter Marie married but had no children.[185] So relax, his genes are extinct—kaput—and will not creep into your neighborhood any time soon. Not even at midnight on the worst full moon Halloween. Although Gilles has been called a precursor to the modern serial killer, it is not fair to blame him for everything that happens. Modern killers would still find a way, even without his trail-blazing efforts.

The name of Gilles de Rais will live in infamy, but some people claim the poor man was framed. They argue that you shouldn't jump to conclusions every time you find a barrel of dead children on someone's property. Alas, the truth will never be known, and that might be a good thing because the less said about Gilles de Rais the better. People like him don't matter and are not worth bothering about. I'm sorry I even brought him up.

Anyway, his life teaches us the importance of good housekeeping. Now can we move on to the next chapter?

---

[185] Goody!

Casanova

Casanova was the world's greatest lover, but what he really wanted was his mama. He pursued women because his mother had deserted him. A fairy godmother would have sufficed as well. Even a nanny would have helped! His grandmother loved him, but she died. Manon Balletti loved him, but by then he was too far gone.

His stormy youth in Venice was marked by typical childish pranks: ringing fire alarm bells, setting gondolas loose, sending midwives to venerable old ladies who were nowhere near pregnant, gang-raping the weaver's wife. Was it his fault that moral standards were at low ebb in 1725, when he was born?

Young Casanova wanted to be a doctor when he grew up because there was money in it, but settled for a law degree at age seventeen. Then he became a cleric, a soldier, a fiddler, a gambler, a coin clipper, a translator, a horoscope reader, a cabalistic con man, an all-purpose scoundrel. He tried practically everything, from honest to dishonest, but had no idea how to support himself in a style befitting his estimation of his importance. He even considered becoming a monk.[186] It was steady, after all, but his vocation left him at the first glimpse of a pretty face. He wanted to be pope, but it didn't work out. Finally he found his true calling: living off the gullible rich while celebrating the rites of Aphrodite with practically everybody and her sister.

At age twenty-one he was adopted by Senator Bragadin, possibly a pederast, who gave him a steady allowance. *Steady* was the operative word. It meant he was relieved of the need to drudge for bread and freed to devote himself full-time to his hobbies: collecting women and letters of introduction.

Casanova did not always succeed in seducing women, but tried so hard and so often that the odds were in his favor. If flattery failed, he tried cash. After all, it was his duty to seduce women; otherwise some insensitive brute would do so. He did his duty, pursuing women wherever they could be found, in all the logical places: brothels, theaters, orgy barns, gambling dens. And in all the illogical places: nunneries, at Mass, at public executions. He would attend weddings hoping to seduce the bride. A damsel in distress always spelled opportunity.

Casanova loved every woman he mated with, but always discovered afterwards that he didn't really mean it. Fate always seemed to intervene in his marriage plans. He never feared that his lovers would leave him; indeed he feared that they would not, because once was enough with most of them. After doing a woman he would decide that he was not worthy of her and fix her up with

---

[186] His general confession took three hours and evoked very pleasant memories.

someone who was. "When the lamp is taken away, all women are alike," he would say. But he was always on the lookout for one who would be different.

Let's face it, Casanova was not the stuff of which husbands are made. He did not want to have and to hold until death and all that, although Henriette tempted him. She must have been something special because their affair lasted for weeks, a record for him. Was it love? Was Casanova capable of true love and commitment? Or was skin-deep good enough for him? We'll get back to that later.

Was he capable of celibacy? Yes, under certain conditions, such as when he was a prisoner of the Inquisition in Venice. But under normal conditions, his "little fellow" was always ready for action. He had no ethical organs, and no one yet has been able to detect a superego in him.

Some have called Casanova a pedophile, but he took on lovers as old as fifty or sixty. Sure he fancied nymphets but, as I said, it was his mama that he wanted. As far as we know, all his lovers were at least ten years old. He drew the line at ten. He thought people made too much fuss about the urge to merge. After all, wasn't it only inevitable?

How did he become the world's greatest lover, the "Great Stallion of Europe?"

    * He was tall, dark, and handsome in his youth. That helped.

    * He gave himself aristocratic titles and pretended to be wealthy.

    * He was adept at the use of flattery, and had cash to spend when flattery failed.

    * He wore a papal order around his neck to impress Catholic women.

    * He curled his hair and wore pomade scented with the essence of whale intestines.

    * He had nerve in infinite amounts.

* He was not at all fussy, being willing to have affairs with old hags, children, humpbacks, trollops, and strumpets. They all counted in the statistics.

* He lived dangerously, having an affair with the mistress of an Inquisitor.

* He was under the special protection of Paralis, his avatar and guardian angel, who unfortunately was helpless against venereal diseases.

* At St. Petersburg he simply purchased a fourteen-year-old serf, although he had to trade her in when she tried to kill him.

* He was a double-dipper. When his prey was guarded by a female chaperon, he would seduce them both.

"All women can be bought," he said, "some with flattery, others with cash." We don't know what Casanova was like in bed but once, when he took on two lovers at a time, the bed collapsed.

Casanova has been criticized for proposing marriage to his daughter Leonilda but, in fairness, he did not know that she was his daughter. Didn't he often encounter children who looked like him? At the coronation of Leopold II in Vienna he saw Leonilda, as well as the son he had with her.[187] It was a family affair, and then some. But he did not carnally possess his nine-year-old daughter Giacomina. Let's give him some credit for that! Endore says that Leonilda may have been a fictional character. Then what about her son?

In Venice the Inquisition decided that Casanova's peccadillos had gone too far and put him into the Leads prison, where he suffered from heat, cold, rats, fleas, hunger, darkness, celibacy, and most of all from having nothing to read but Sister Mary's pious book "The Mystical City." This book eventually drove him to

---

[187] Incest was a venial sin in those days. A few fervent Hail Marys and you were good to go.

desperation and he escaped, which made him a celebrity.[188] Then followed years of exile from Venice.

Casanova was one of the three top quacks of his time. The others, Counts Saint-Germain and Cagliostro, had a hard time keeping up with him. In Holland, a banker's daughter named Esther wanted Casanova to initiate her into his cabalistic science, but how could he? It did not exist. She did not exist either, according to Endore. But police records prove that Casanova existed.

One of Casanova's benefactors was Madam d'Urfe, one of the great nuts of all time. Born to be duped, she wanted to possess the philospher's stone, whatever that was. Since only males could possess it, she wanted to be reborn into a male body. No problem, said Casanova, who devised a plan. When it did not work out, he advised her to write to Selinis, the man in the moon. When Selinis did not respond, Casanova referred her to his friends in the Milky Way. About 1763 she finally came to her senses and learned to live without the silly rock, but the million francs she gave Casanova were gone, never to return. Casanova felt he must cheat the gullible or someone else would. He was addicted to her money and felt that since it was destined to be spent on follies anyway, why not make it pay for his?

Casanova traveled widely—he *had* to! Often he had to leave towns in a hurry, by way of walls, because there were complaints about him: that he won too consistently at the gaming tables or at the game of love. He left behind a trail of unpaid debts and abandoned lovers. Banished from most of the major cities of Europe, he soon ran out of places where he could pursue his scams. At Vienna the chastity commission took a lively interest in him. He considered relocating to Madagascar. It is a wonder he did not go to America!

---

[188] Casanova's account of his imprisonment and escape is recommended to prudes and prigs who would like to read him without having to wash afterwards.

Casanova was not harmless. There were the VD epidemics he caused and the plague of bastards he scattered around Europe. But he tried not to beat up women, unless they were tarts or otherwise deserved it. The death of that nun at Aix-en-Savoie was an accident. Why bring that up? How was Casanova to know that she couldn't handle that much opium? And didn't his dueling opponents usually survive their injuries?

Casanova said that he tried to make women happy, but his treatment of women would not meet today's higher standards. He got his revenge against one tart in London by teaching a parrot to call her a whore. This would be politically incorrect today. She reportedly bought the cheeky bird and had it strangled.

Casanova had a remarkable sense of humor. He once cut off the arm of a freshly-buried corpse and presented it to a sleeping man during the night from under his bed. The poor man did not take it well. He had a stroke and was never the same after that, but it was a jolly good joke, wasn't it?

Casanova loved Venice because of the wantonness of its women, but Venice did not love him back. His fondest wish was to be allowed to go home, and it was finally granted in 1774. He returned, on probation, under the watchful eyes of the local Inquisitors. He tried to behave himself, and even worked as a spy and moral agent for the Inquisition. Yes, moral agent! You heard me right! Sure it was a stretch for him, of all people, to be enforcing public morality, but the poor man had to make a living somehow.[189] In the end, Venice did not work out, because he was still Casanova. By 1783, he was banished and on the road again.

Then Count Waldstein gave him a job as librarian in his castle in Bohemia. In this bleak, godforsaken place, Casanova wrote his memoirs, which are read to this day

---

[189] He was accused of giving away state secrets, but I don't believe it. He would have sold them!

by Casanovists and dirty old men. Havelock Ellis said that Casanova was a consummate master in the dignified narration of undignified experiences. The memoirs end rather abruptly in 1774 because, quite frankly, his life after that was a bore. He had to behave himself in Venice, which does not make for good reading.

Too old to make himself ill in his favorite way, Casanova turned to gluttony. He wanted to suck life dry, in one way or another. He never did find Ms. Right or a fairy godmother, but there at Dux in Bohemia, he finally found a true soul-mate, a wire-haired terrier bitch named Melampyge.[190] So you see, he *was* capable of true love after all! And even commitment! He saw Melampyge with the eyes of the soul. His poetry to her gushed with such sentiment that it had to be written in Latin![191] But alas, poor Melampyge died of despair, admitted Casanova, because he would not allow her to mate. Could he help it that he couldn't find another dog worthy of her? She was fussy! Was that the real reason, or did he fear a love triangle? Was our man consumed by jealousy? After a decorous period of grieving, he had an affair with a foxy terrier named Finette. I'm not making this up!

Painfully aware of his humble origins, Casanova wanted respect, so he gave himself a title: Chevalier de Seingalt. I don't know where Seingalt was, he probably didn't know himself, but it *sounds* good, doesn't it? Casanova was a nobleman because he *said* he was. He didn't wait to have nobility conferred upon him. That would have been too long a wait. Besides, hadn't he dueled with nobles and shared venereal diseases with nobles on a level of equality? Hadn't he fired a bullet into the august body of the lord marshal of Poland? Hadn't he corrected Voltaire? Fifteen of his lovers were blue-blooded, according to his memoirs. Eighteen were

---

[190] There are some who question whether Melampyge was a she. It is a bit late now to check on that.
[191] Good thing the memoirs end before this episode!

wealthy gentlewomen. One was even a theologian! But despite his efforts to become famous and respected, he had to settle for being infamous and suspected.

Although he once beat up a publisher for calling him an adventurer, Casanova wrote poetry under the name of Eupolemo Pantareno![192] He also answered to Count Farussi, Antonio Pratolini, Paralis Blacksnout, and Mr. Cornelis. At Chiaggia he was known as "the Prince of Macaroni" because of the verses he composed in praise of that noble pasta. But Boswell called him a blockhead.

Casanova was a man of many talents:
* He could tell a good story, whether or not it was true.
* He knew the pawning value of everything.
* He could make the pope laugh, and did so.
* He was good at giving moral advice to others.
* He could make love to women who did not exist, and even catch VD from them. [193]
* If his memoirs are to be believed, he could be in two places at one time.
But none of these paid steadily.

The Prince de Ligne said that Casanova was good company, if you didn't mind his perpetual quotations from Horace and Homer, and his incessant chatter about magic, cabalism, macaroni, and little girls. Casanova was paranoid about Jacobins, but was very generous, especially to impotent male friends who wanted or needed heirs. Although he has been called a rake from hell, he was not all bad. He found suitable husbands for many women and brought prosperity to doctors who treated venereal diseases. Casanova probably has many descendants alive today, but they hardly ever mention him. They don't seem to be interested.

---

[192] Not a typo.
[193] You ask, how many times did Casanova catch VD? Eleven times that we know of.

Some say Casanova was bisexual, others say he was omnisexual. His life teaches us that if there is no quality in your life, try quantity. Try excess. *Sequere Deum,* his rule of life, meant to follow your bliss. He followed his bliss all over Europe, but never quite caught up with it. His stats do not always measure up to modern standards—Elvis Presley claimed more lovers, for example. But remember, Casanova had no fan clubs or groupies to help out. He didn't even know what a teenybopper was!

He said that "opportunity is like fortune: one must seize it by the forelock as soon as it appears or it will run away and not return." He felt much the same about women.

Hetty Green

Pity poor Hetty Green, in her tattered and worn dowdy black clothing, subsisting alone in shabby unfurnished rooms on cold oatmeal and graham crackers. Clipping coupons day in and day out. Her only companion a canine of no particular distinction.

What's that you say? Hetty Green had sufficient means to live uptown? At the "Y" perhaps? Well golly gee! Can it be true? It says here that in 1865 she inherited millions of Yankee dollars from her auntie and her father. Then why the show of poverty? Was she hiding out from tax collectors? Lawyers? Robbers? Assassins? All of the above? She wasn't fooling anybody. All the bankers on Wall Street knew her. Newspaper reporters followed her around. Songs were written about her.

Despite appearances, Hetty Green was not really down or out. She always had a home at the Chemical National Bank, where her money lived in splendor. Bankers pampered her, as she could have created instant panic by drawing out her funds. The coupons she clipped were from bonds. She was swamped by them.

Hetty Robinson was born in New Bedford, Massachusetts, in 1834, of parsimonious Quaker stock. Her father, a world-class miser, was a connoisseur of free lunches. (There were still free lunches in those days.) Her great-grandfather, Isaac Howland, was an oil millionaire. No, not that kind of oil, whale oil, from blubber.[194] Her mother and her auntie inherited his money. As luck would have it, Auntie Sylvia was a withered old spinster and Hetty's only sibling died in infancy, so Hetty had it figured out from way back that she was in line for the Howland goodies. It used to drive her nuts to see her auntie and her parents frittering away her inheritance. She tried in vain to teach them thrift. Would there be anything left for her? She vowed not to spend it when it finally became hers because it wasn't spending money she wanted but capital. She wanted to play the game of capitalism. She wanted to compound her compound interest. She wanted to buy low and sell high. She was as hard-nosed as any man when money was involved. In short, she was greedy, and could smell a bull market all the way from Hoboken!

It helped a lot when her father died in 1865. He left her a cool million,[195] but tied up in trust, so Hetty could not get her hot little hands on most of it. So near and yet so far! Still, he left her more than enough cash to begin playing the game and she started buying greenbacks. They were quite affordable back then, just after the Civil War. Then Aunt Sylvia finally went defunct, leaving Hetty more assets to play with, but also tied up in trust.[196] There was still a lot of litigating to do before the real fun could

---

[194] I'm not going to mention that Hetty was introduced to the Prince of Wales as the Princess of Whales because I don't do puns. Well, hardly ever!

[195] Has there ever been a million that wasn't cool?

[196] Hetty went into mourning when Auntie died. Not for Auntie, but for the provisions of her will.

begin, but she bought Civil War bonds, more greenbacks, mortgages, rail stock, and watched them sprout. She owned no factories and produced no gizmos,[197] but her assets grew like crabgrass on a suburban lawn.

Hetty had to flee to England for a while—something about a forgery charge—but returned when the statute of limitations expired. By 1872 her money was in the clear and by 1884 she was worth $26 million and at least a footnote in the history of Wall Street.

Hetty's financial education began in childhood. At the docks she accompanied her father on his rounds of his whaling ships.[198] Then at Dr. Lowell's Finishing School she was taught well, perhaps too well, that thrift was a virtue and waste a vice. She never forgot, and carried her tattered old Bible in her tattered old black bag or her tattered old pockets, along with her graham crackers, yesterday's ham sandwich, a raw onion, and her pistol. No, she didn't splurge to buy the gun; it was a gift from fans in California. She carried it for protection against lawyers. She detested lawyers, but somehow married one. They had a pre-nuptial agreement: he would be the family breadwinner and she would be free to pursue her hobby on Wall Street. What was hers was not to be his. Somehow they had two children who were hardly liquid assets.

When Hubby's fortune plunged into the basement in 1885, she dumped him like a stock at its apogee. Despite their pre-nuptial agreement, his debts contaminated her stash and he became a huge, sucking, liability. He was no use to her, she said. She could pay for her own graham crackers, thank you, by buying them in bulk. She had little in common with Hubby anyhow, as he was a generous tipper who liked high living and expensive

---

[197] It is not surprising that she produced no gizmos, as the word had not yet been invented.
[198] Hetty could cuss like a sailor. Her vocabulary was bigger than a Quaker lady's ought to be.

clothes. They often quarreled—about money, of course. What else?

Some say that Hetty's stinginess passed beyond harmless eccentricity when her son Ned hurt his knee sledding. In order to spare the cost of a doctor, the story goes, she treated it herself, with warm sand, baked onions, and tobacco leaves. It didn't work out, and Ned's leg had to be amputated. His cork prosthesis cost more than a doctor would have. She blew it and knew it!

Hetty was not entirely friendless. Countess Annie Leary put up with her and tried to get her to loosen up a bit on her purse strings, but in vain. Hetty's best friend was her dog, Cupid Dewey.[199] She liked him because he was not a lawyer. Sometimes she called herself Mrs. Dewey, but there is no evidence that they were ever married.[200] Marriage with Dewey would not have worked out anyway, because he did not care about money. A Skye terrier, Dewey earned his beefsteaks and rice pudding by keeping lawyers and assassins at bay. He had to beg for his food, but ate better than she did. Apparently Dewey managed her business affairs as well because when he died in 1910, Hetty had to ask her son Ned to come up from Texas to take over the job. Hetty once moved out of New Jersey to avoid paying a two dollar state dog tax. It was not the money, it was the principle of the thing. It was not fair to tax her prime minister as if he were nothin' but a houn' daug. Her daughter finally paid the two dollars.

Hetty Green gave us these common sense tips:

* Return berry baskets for the deposit.
* Send letters collect.
* If you must splurge on cookies, buy broken ones. They taste just as good.
* Cook on radiators to save gas.

---

[199] Named after Admiral Dewey.
[200] "C. Dewey" was the official name on her mailbox.

* Who needs hot water?

* Buying fripperies is wicked, even if the price is right.

* Wear black clothing. It doesn't show dirt. Launder only the dirty parts of clothing, such as the bottom hems that drag on the ground.

* Never eat out, except at Pie Alley. Eat slowly. Buy soup that is thick on the bottom. Never tip anyone unless they are nicer than Santa Claus, and then only a nickel. Haggle over prices. Throw tantrums, as needed.

* Don't maintain an office. It costs money and tells assassins, deadbeats, and tax collectors where to find you.

* Don't trust suitors or bankers, especially good-looking ones. Don't trust men who smile too much. Watch out for Robin Hoods; they are lurking everywhere.

* Try not to have children, but if they do show up, teach them thrift. Then put them to work for you.

* Teach your parents thrift.

* Never own an automobile. An ass was good enough for Jesus.

* Inherit millions. Then buy low and sell high.

Hetty believed in holding on to real estate, but not developing it because that would raise taxes. Her policy was just to let it age slowly, like vintage wine, to fiscal perfection. But her tenement buildings did not age to perfection; they rotted into slums. You wouldn't want Hetty for a landlady! She didn't do leaky faucets.

It is not true that Hetty wanted to buy the Chicago Cubs baseball franchise, as she was partial to winners. For some reason, the Cubs reminded her of a bear market.

There has been much speculation about what was in Hetty's little black satchel. Was it hundreds of thousands in bonds? Was it precious jewels? Was it a fortune in cash? Or was it her lunch? Frankly, I don't know. Probably her Bible. She knew her Bible well, except for the part about the camel passing through the eye of a needle. She kept bonds in her bosom—don't ask me how I know. And her remarkable petticoat had more pockets than a periodontal basket case. Enough pockets to stash the Comstock Lode, they say.

What do you think? Did Hetty Green overdo the thrift game with her petty economies? Should she have added raisins to her oatmeal? On special occasions, at least? Did she really need more flowers on her bonnet?

Was she a liberated woman who beat men at their own game? A financial wizard? Or was she a cold-hearted, stingy witch? She didn't care that her black clothing made her look like a witch. Think of the money she saved on laundry bills.

Hetty's wardrobe was not up-to-date, but it may not be strictly true that she changed lawyers more often than she changed her clothing.[201] It is arguable. No doubt she was a frump and a slattern, but it helped her get things for free. She didn't like paying on a sliding scale—or any other scale, for that matter.

Hetty paid for a pistol permit because she feared "unbalanced" people. She had separation anxiety about her money. Would modern medications have helped? Probably not, as she would have found their costs "prohibitive." Was Hetty Green insane? The jury is still out on that one. Was she happy? She would have found the question impertinent. What good is happiness? It won't buy you money. But money can make you wealthy. Hetty Green could not vote but, no matter, neither did she have to pay income taxes. In a plutocracy like ours, money counts for more than votes. She had no cause for complaint. She called herself "a poor, lone woman with no political voice," but her money would not shut up.

To no one's surprise, Hetty Green died as rich as sin. Her playboy son Ned claimed that she was a closet philanthropist who gave away millions, but people tend to see good in their mothers, even when it isn't there. Her will left nothing to charity. Practically everything went to Ned and her nondescript daughter Sylvia. She wanted to keep it in the family, as there were not many people Hetty trusted, and most of them were dogs. Ned said his mother was misunderstood. Indeed there are many fables and

---

[201] Hetty wore an indestructable black dress that gradually turned brown, then green. Most historians now believe that it was originally black—when it was new, if it ever was.

myths about Hetty Green, as nothing stimulates talk like big money combined with world-class weirdness.

Hetty Green was "economic in the most elaborate sense of the word," said the *New York Times*. She was the world's greatest miser, said the *Guinness Book of World Records*. Not bad for someone who was not even trying. I guess she was a natural. She got in at the bottom and out at the top, and made it look easy. Whenever she wrote a check, she could feel a piece of her flesh being torn away.

She died worth $100 million—some say $200 million, no one knows for sure. Her fortune did not approach that of Scrooge McDuck, of course, but she did alright, for a girl. Or did she? Was it Cupid Dewey, not Hetty, who was the brains in the family? We will never know for sure. Anyway, she proved that an unproductive person can do just fine in our economic system. Indeed, she is an inspiration to unproductive people everywhere.

Hetty's life teaches us that, rich or poor, it's nice to have money. Even if you never spend it, it cheers things up considerably.

Rasputin

Rasputin was known as "the Mad Monk," although he was not a monk. A Siberian peasant who could barely read or write, he became the ruler of one-sixth of the earth and proved that a deranged peasant could make mistakes as well as the most professional of politicians.

But Rasputin's morals were the talk of the town. His brains were located below his waist and were soluble in alcohol. People thought him too friendly to pretty young women. He would kiss them on the lips and stroke their bosoms to be friendly. It was his way of introducing himself. He liked to test the virtue of young girls by inviting them to sleep with him. Was it his fault if some of them flunked? He liked to take baths with them, even when they were not dirty.[202]

Either you like Rasputin or you don't. To his female followers he was a saint and a love machine. To his male critics he was a loathsome reptile. The truth lies somewhere in between. He was not all bad. He was like Robin Hood; he stole kisses from the rich and gave them to the poor. Horses liked him.

In his youth, Rasputin was called *Soplyak* or "Snot-nosed kid." He grew up into a snot-nosed Siberian peasant who chased girls, got drunk, and ate with his fingers. He smoked tobacco, picked quarrels, got married, and made babies, not necessarily in that order. Rasputin loved his wife. The problem was that he loved all the young women in Siberia. And they loved him back. Sometimes he would get drunk with his father. Then they would beat up each other. They were a close family. Rasputin had a hard time behaving himself, but don't we all? As a youth he went to a monastery, hoping to get his life in order, and came back changed. Actually, he came back unhinged.

He had a gift of prophecy, in addition to his obvious gift of debauchery. He was said to be inspired, but with what? There was something in his viper-green eyes. Was it the Holy Spirit? They say he could hypnotize a rock, but how could they tell? Some called him a horse thief, which hardly seems fair, as horses were drawn to him like rats to the Pied Piper.

One day the Virgin of Kazan appeared to Rasputin, and a thousand angels singing celestial music. Well, it was impressive! It made him want to reform his wayward life, but how? Sexual restraint was contrary to his nature. After all, he was well endowed, like the proverbial Greek.

---

[202] Rasputin took no interest in older women, even when they needed a bath. But he bathed young women "in beatitude," said Anna Vyrubova, one of his more mindless disciples.

Thirteen inches erect, according to his daughter Maria—above average for a saint. Big enough to get 57,600 links on Google. What was it for? Wouldn't it be a sin to waste such a gift of God by being celibate? Luckily he found a religious sect that taught sexual degradation as the way to salvation. It sounded good to him so he became fanatically holy.

According to the legend, Rasputin wandered around Russia accompanied by a band of female disciples who had left husbands and parents to follow him. Their religious rites included debaucheries that cannot be mentioned in a family essay such as this one. You'll have to use your imaginations. He claimed supernatural powers of clairvoyance, exorcism, prophecy, healing. He could cure the most stubborn cases of virginity in women, but only in young women. His healing powers did not work at all on older women, or so he claimed. (He never actually bothered to try on older women.) Dried up old hags couldn't sin if they tried, he thought, and sin was necessary to his program. Sin + repentence = redemption. That was how it worked. As repentance was necessary for redemption, one needed something to repent. So, after repenting one's sins, all the way down to the venial ones, it was necessary to go out and commit some more, to create the necessary conditions for more repentence. The more sins the more repentence the more redemption. Got it? Think of all the redemption you could pile up for a rainy day if you could sin vigorously enough![203]

The greatest obstacle to salvation was pride, and the remedy was humiliation through sexual degradation. Rasputin made self-debasement fashionable. Bored women of high birth sought it as a new sensation. It became chic. Everybody wanted to try debasing themselves, for God and country.

---

[203] You could even sell any surplus redemption.

Rasputin admitted that he debased women, but it was for their own spiritual good. For innocent young things who did not know how to debase themselves, he was there to help out. He initiated hordes of them into bizarre sexual rituals, remitting their sins by taking them upon himself. Then he would recycle the sins. He liked to cast demons out of nuns, if they were young and good-looking (the nuns, that is; not the demons).

His disciples were appreciative beyond the call of duty. They liked to sew silk blouses for him, brush his hair, and give him baths. If they were lucky he might let them launder his dirty linen or clip his nails and keep the clippings, which were prized relics. They saw profundity in his unintelligible chatter. His illegible scrawls were holy writ to them.

He was onto a good thing and didn't he know it? So he took his show on the road, to the capital, St. Petersburg, where Czar Nicholas was frantically searching for someone to tell him what to do. Nicky had a habit of seeking out fools, idiots, and imbeciles for counsel in political affairs, and then along came Rasputin.

Soon Czarina Alexandra was sewing silk blouses for Rasputin. She became his most celebrated disciple. She believed he had access to the Almighty.[204] Just gazing at his photograph was healing. Even his comb had special powers. If the czar merely ran it through the imperial hair, it would give him courage and wisdom, if not cooties. She held Rasputin in such reverence that she even capitalized pronouns that referred to Him![205] Surely he could relieve the suffering of her son Alexei, who was ill with hemophilia. The sick boy did seem to respond, and soon Rasputin was making himself at home in the imperial palace, eating well and addressing the czar and

---

[204] Rasputin often chatted with Saints Peter and Paul and the Virgin of Kazan. They even chatted back.
[205] According to the University of Chicago, even God is not entitled to uppercased pronouns.

czarina as "Papa" and "Mama." He was like family, or so he thought. And what did the czar think? According to his mother, Nicholas was too pure of heart to see evil in anything—even when it moved in and made itself at home.

Meanwhile Rasputin's lecherous exploits were the talk of St. Petersburg and it was considered indecent to have anything to do with him. He was a superstar of sorts, known around town as "that awful man." People locked up their women when he was in the neighborhood. You should have seen the graffiti! Everyone tried to pretend they didn't know him, including the czar, who tried sending him home to Siberia. But he kept coming back. Rasputin felt he had outgrown Siberia.

Finally the czar forbade any mention of Rasputin in the press, under penalty of a fine. But the papers gladly paid the fine because his antics were hot copy. Some of the police reports were considered "too vile" to release to the public. When presented with lewd photos of Rasputin carousing with naked women, the czar decided to send him on pilgrimage to the Holy Land. But, of course, he came back.

The czarina preferred not to believe the rumors about Rasputin. He always behaved himself around her, except for that time when he seduced her children's nurse. But why bring that up? To date there is no evidence that Rasputin ever messed around with the czarina. Never mind the gossip. She was too old for him anyway. He did not have an Oedipus complex. He even called her "the old woman."

Rasputin became an indispensable nuisance to the imperial family, an official personage with his own staff and his own limousine, which could go faster than police cars. He would nag and browbeat the poor czar, who would run and hide from him to avoid granting his requests.

Rasputin's flat in St. Petersburg was a busy place. Here he received female petitioners who wanted him to intercede for them with the czar, or with the Holy Spirit. He took them into a bedroom he called "the Holy of Holies," to talk business and have "religious" experiences. There was a rear exit through the kitchen for hasty retreats when irate husbands came to the front door brandishing revolvers. Other petitioners preferred to leave by the front door, clutching their clothing and screaming "rape!" Some women went into a swoon when Rasputin gazed into their eyes. They should have went into a taxi!

Rasputin's enemies could easily get him into trouble by providing three basic ingredients: pretty women, Madeira wine, and gypsy music. They would alert the media and he would do the rest. His arrival at a party always attracted a crowd and the police would send for reinforcements. He liked to take off his clothes and dance naked for high society ladies and government officials. It was all part of his religion. Sometimes he got so religious he had to be carried home.

When Czar Nicholas went away to the Great War, Rasputin and the czarina were left in charge of the empire. The czar received instructions by telegram from his wife. Guess where she got them. Rasputin was Russia's secret weapon, proof that God was on their side. So what if the Germans had airplanes? Airplanes indeed! She was confident of victory. After all, Nicky had Rasputin's comb with him at the front to give him wisdom and to strengthen his resolve.

Meanwhile, back in the capital, colleagues preferred to do business with Rasputin in the morning hours. Because of his fondness for vodka and Madeira wine, he could not be relied upon to be coherent after lunch. Sometimes they had to pick up the tab for his meals. Sometimes they had to pick up Rasputin himself from the floor. When drunk he sometimes spilled state secrets, as well as vodka. His eating habits also were sufficient to make him a legend. A waiter complained that he "grabbled" his food. He ate soup with his fingers, said Pares. He didn't use napkins; that's what his beard was for.

When filling important government jobs, Rasputin had no use for work histories or résumés. He relied on intuition, simply gazing into the eyes of applicants until he had penetrated to the bottoms of their souls. In this way he removed many fools from important government positions and replaced them with idiots. He liked to give important jobs to his drinking companions, but only if they believed in God. He made such a mess of things that some people thought he was working for the Germans.

Rasputin believed in autocracy because the autocrats fed him and the Duma did not. But his antics made the autocrats look even sillier than they actually were. He was considered a malignancy at the heart of the state and a threat to the throne. So ignoble nobles did him in, which was known in the vernacular as "removing the filth." It did no good, as there was still a lot of filth left. Czar Nicholas punished the murderers by banishment to pleasant places where they could enjoy themselves, write books about the murder, and be safe from the revolution that soon followed. One of them paid his debt to society by selling champagne in Palm Beach, Florida.

In a different setting, Rasputin might have been relatively harmless. Like a hippie, he wanted to make love not war, but he could have done it longer if he'd had sense enough to stay in Siberia.

About Sources

I read the standard biographies recommended by the major encyclopedias, plus many background books, mostly histories, and reference books such as the Dictionary of American Biography. Histories included those of the East India Company, the French Revolution, the South African diamond industry, the Standard Oil Company, Italian Fascism, various wars, and many others. Plus biographies of secondary characters such as Joan of Arc, Isabella d'Este, Queen Elizabeth I, George Francis Train, Czar Nicholas II, and Manuel Azana. Political science by George Seldes and Niccolo Machiavelli. Published letters and diaries by Pietro Bembo and Lucretia Borgia, Queen Victoria, Hernan Cortes, Count Galeazzo Ciano, Eva Braun, Adolf Hitler and his doctor. Published interviews with John D. Rockefeller and Benito Mussolini. Other sources included audiotapes, television documentaries, Book TV, magazines such as LIFE, Horizon, and McClure's. Periodicals such as the New York Times, the Guardian, the New England Quarterly, North American Review, Journal of American History, Political Science Quarterly. Autobiographies tend to be biased, but I did cautiously read a few personal memoirs, including those of Casanova, U. S. Grant, Julia Dent Grant, and Kaiser Wilhelm. I read Hitler's *Mein Kampf* and Anthony Comstock's *Traps for the Young*. I avoided fictional accounts and made cautious use of a few Internet sources. This book was thoroughly researched; its bibliography is too big for the space available here. Many sources are cited within the text.

—PJS

Picture Sources

Bismarck
* Caricature by Felix Regamey (1844-1907)
* Cartoon by Thomas Nast, *Harper's Weekly,* 13 Feb. 1886

Borgias
* Alexander VI, from an engraving dated 1580
* Lucretia Borgia, from a painting in Musee de Nimes

Casanova
* Engraving by Johann Berka (1758-1815), from a portrait by Jacob Hieron

Clive
* Mezzotint by James McArdell (1729-1765), after Gainsborough
* From an oil painting by Francis Hayman, circa 1760

Comstock
* Cartoon from *New York World,* 7 Jan. 1898
* Cartoon from *Life,* 1 November 1906

Cortes
* By Gabriel Lobo Lasso de la Vega, Madrid, 1588

Cromwell
* *Zigzag Journeys in Europe,* 1879
* A. M. Richards, from *Bill Nye's Comic History of England,* 1906

Gilles de Rais
* By Manuel Ferran (1835-1896)
* Joan of Arc from *Bill Nye's Comic History of England,* 1906

Grant
* *The Century War Book,* 1884
* Thomas Nast, *Harper's Weekly,* 17 March 1877
* *Perley's Reminiscences Illustrated,* 1886

Hearst
* From *Collier's Weekly,* September 1906
* From a cartoon by J. S. Pughe, *Puck,* 1904

Hitler
* Photos.com

Inquisition
* Tomas Bertran Soler, Valencia, 1858
* Torquemada by Juan Barcelone after Jose Maea (1790-1826)
* Hartmann Schedel, *Liber Chronicarum,* 1493

Ivan the Terrible
* German engraving, 16th century, Bibliotheque Nationale, Paris
* Slavonic Division, New York Public Library

Jackson
* Campaign cartoon circa 1832

Kaiser Wilhelm
* From a cartoon by Gabriele Galantara (1865-1937), *l'Asino,* 11 Oct. 1914
* Cartoon by Edmund Joseph Sullivan (1869-1933), 1915

Marie Antoinette
* F. H. Drouais (1727-1775)
* Claude-Louis Desrais (1746-1816)
* James Gillray (1756-1815)

Mussolini
* From a cartoon by George Whitelaw (1887-1957) published in the *Daily Herald,* London, 12 June 1940. Reproduced by permission from Mirrorpix.

Napoleon
* Bibliotheque Nationale, Paris
* Color engraving by Anonymous, 1815

Pirates
* American School, from *History of the Most Notorious Pyrates*, 1725
* From *Historie der Engelsche Zee-roovers*, 1725

Ralegh
* From *Historie of the World*, 1634
* A. M. Richards, from *Bill Nye's Comic History of England*, 1906

Rasputin
* Caricature face by By N. Ivanov, 1916

Rhodes
* From *L'Assiette au Beurre*, 28 September 1901
* From *Le Rire*, Paris, 14 February 1900

Rockefeller
* Cartoon entitled *King of Combinations*, artist unknown
* Carlo de Fornaro, from *Mortals and Immortals*, 1911

Tweed
* From a cartoon by Thomas Nast, *Harper's Weekly*, 19 Jan. 1878
* Thomas Nast, *Harper's Weekly*, 23 Dec. 1871

Victoria
* From *Fun*, 1 July 1891
* From *Le Rire*, Paris, 1899

Woodrow Wilson
* Caricature by E. Hine, 1912
* Artist unknown, 1912

About the Author

P. J. Sullivan studied history at Saint Louis University and in the field in more than a dozen countries, including Spain, where he had close encounters with Franco's finest. After five years of total immersion in Europe and North Africa, he returned to the States in 1973 and became a columnist and cartoonist for progressive causes. Drawn to the past, he has co-authored a book of genealogy and edited a book of Civil War letters from Missouri. Since 1975 he has been based in Humboldt County, California.